2002
508

DINNER AFTER DARK

COLIN COWIE
DINNER AFTER DARK

SEXY, SUMPTUOUS SUPPER SOIRÉES

PHOTOGRAPHS BY QUENTIN BACON

CLARKSON POTTER / PUBLISHERS

NEW YORK

Grateful acknowledgment is made to: Maya Kaimal MacMillan, for permission
to reprint the recipe for Stir-Fried Shrimp with Lemon and Scallions on
page 115 from her book *Curried Favors,* copyright © 1996; Rani, for
permission to reprint the recipes for Peach Chutney on page 108,
Mango Chutney on page 117, and Garam Masala on page 119 from her
book *Feast of India,* copyright © 1991; and Nellie & Joe's, for permission
to reprint their recipe for Key Lime Pie on page 150.

Published by Clarkson Potter/Publishers, New York. New York.
Member of the Crown Publishing Group, a division of Random House, Inc.
www.randomhouse.com

CLARKSON N. POTTER is a trademark and POTTER and colophon
are registered trademarks of Random House, Inc.

Printed in China

Design by Shahid & Company

Photographs by Quentin Bacon

Library of Congress Cataloging-in-Publication Data
Cowie, Colin, 1962–
Dinner after dark: sexy, sumptuous supper soirées / Colin Cowie;
photographs by Quentin Bacon.
I. Dinners and dining.   2. Entertaining.   I. Title.
TX737 .c654   2002
642'.4—dc21   2001057790

ISBN 0-609-60975-0

10 9 8 7 6 5 4 3 2 1

First Edition

Contents

INTRODUCTION

For me, one of life's greatest pleasures is inviting guests into my home to dine. I love entertaining. I love to set a beautiful table, relax over a cocktail, and cook a simple, delicious meal. Through my books and television programs, I feel privileged to share this pleasure with my many friends, clients, readers, and viewers so that they too can experience the joy of entertaining in style.

We live in a fast-paced world under a seemingly limitless barrage of information. Cell phones, faxes, and E-mails raise communications to a fever pitch. Time seems to be measured in nanoseconds. There's a constant demand for split-second answers and instantaneous decisions. I've never been busier and I'm always on the move. When I'm in town, though, I try to cook dinner four or five nights a week, and entertain friends as much as possible. I feel strongly that time spent with friends and family around the dinner table, sharing food and laughter, is the most precious of all. When the candles have burned down, the wine bottle is close to empty, and we've spent the last few hours reveling in one another's company, I'll often sit back in my chair, savor the moment, and think, "This is what it's all about!"

Finding the time to entertain can be a challenge. Whether you're dining family style with platters lining the center of the table or sipping wine in the kitchen while dinner is bubbling away in the oven, or perhaps eating from trays while watching a great movie in the den, the goal is to produce a tasty meal that's as quick and easy to prepare as it is good to eat. People mistakenly think entertaining means slaving for days in the kitchen. They feel pressured to do everything themselves—and to do it "perfectly." It's due to this misconception that so many people shy away from inviting friends over. They've been led to believe that if they don't go out to the yard and hand-pick 150 exquisitely tree-ripened cherries to make a perfect pie, it's not worth doing at all! They don't realize that entertaining can be simultaneously easy, chic, and fun. All it takes is some basic skills and know-how, which is exactly what I aim to provide in this book.

Each person has a different style, and no one style is better than another. I have friends I love to visit because they play the latest, hottest music all evening and serve the best grilled-cheese sandwiches in the city. Another friend makes fabulous restaurant-quality desserts. Yet another hates to cook but loves superb Indian takeout.

In each case, what counts is getting together for some quality time. It's not so important where the food comes from or what it is, as long as it's good. The more you entertain, the more comfortable you'll become with the process, and the more your own unique style will emerge. And the more you'll be able to fill your free time with interesting, engaging people who will enrich your life.

It's no fun to host a party if I can't relax and enjoy it with my guests. I have arrived at parties, knocked on the door, and after a long pause been greeted by a host or hostess wearing an apron covered with more ingredients than made it into the salad dressing, looking like he or she had just run six times around the block. They herd you into the living room, thrust a cocktail into your hand, then disappear into the kitchen only to make brief appearances between courses. It's clear that they're not having fun. And the worst of it is that before they know it, their guests will have gone home and all they will have to look forward to is a pile of dishes.

If you have the ability to cook a complicated, multicourse menu entirely from scratch, that's terrific, and more power to you. But what's important to most people is to have a variety of easy recipes and reliable food resources at their fingertips, so that even on short notice they can pull together a delicious dinner and organize a memorable occasion around it.

I've learned over the years how to plan menus that are appropriate for the occasion and to work within the amount of time available, even when it's a busy weeknight. I've developed a simple, foolproof formula: exciting drinks, tasty food, interesting conversation, a good mix of music, a relaxed host, and the proper timing add up to success in entertaining.

It doesn't hurt to have a signature style of cuisine. I grew up in central and southern Africa and was exposed early on to what I call the original "fusion cuisine"—a wide-ranging and delectable blend of ethnic influences. Many of my favorite dishes incorporate the exotic spices and assertive flavors of Africa, the Middle East, and southern Asia. They are not complicated to prepare, and for this book I've simplified the long-cooking stews and many other traditional dishes of these cuisines so that you can try them at home even on short notice.

The goal of this book is to provide successful recipes for the *whole* party—not just directions for preparing the food, but an entire spectrum of inspiration, suggestions, hints, and procedures. Each chapter is not just a meal, but rather a blueprint for a special evening planned around a meal, from appetizer to main course and through dessert. I've taken into account which flavors and recipes complement one another as well as the amounts of time required to shop for, prepare, and serve the dishes. Each of these menus is chic and delicious, fun and exciting, yet simple enough to prepare anytime. In each chapter, I offer ideas for setting the table and creating the right ambience as well as suggestions for matching cocktails and wines.

But there's more than just recipes. The keys to entertaining with casual, effortless elegance are simplicity and advance planning and preparation. I aim to provide you with not only plenty of sizzle and snap, but also with a lot of practical information and suggestions, including shortcuts and built-in escape valves to eliminate pressure. Special features called "411" (an information call) offer background on a particular ingredient or artifact; meanwhile, "911"s (emergency calls) provide "bail-out options" for when you feel like hitting the panic button. On the other hand, "OTT" (Over the Top) features are for when you're feeling especially ambitious, magnanimous, or simply fabulous; they are quick touches that take the party immediately to a higher plane. And finally, while the cuisines I'm providing are generally healthy, simple, and relatively light, the features entitled "A Lighter Touch" offer suggestions for reducing calorie counts.

My approach to entertaining, as embodied in this book, is streamlined, efficient, and, most of all, fun. The formulas work for me on a regular basis, and they'll work for you, too. Just remember: Don't be overly ambitious, and always work within your abilities. Go out and find the best ingredients possible, then do as little to them as possible. Do the work in advance so you can be a guest at your own party. You should be glued to a dining room chair, not chained to the kitchen stove. And remember: You get no medals for making everything from scratch. If the baker down the street makes a better apple pie than you do, don't be ashamed—buy his. Your guests always deserve the best. And no matter who made the dessert, they'll be touched that you've taken the time and put forth the effort to entertain them in style.

Have fun and enjoy!

WELCOME!
FOR 6

This was an elegant celebration to mark a special occasion, yet it was pulled together rather quickly. What were we celebrating? Well, there are a ton of good excuses: birthday, going away, coming home, book publication, successful completion of a project. In this case, it was the launch of a collection of china I had designed.

I think for most people the thought of planning a dinner party for six at short notice is daunting. In fact, they might prefer to skip the whole ordeal. Here's a way to pull it off, mark the occasion with an exclamation point, and still enjoy your own party.

When I first moved into my New York apartment and had the walls painted with liquid copper leaf, I got the notion to create a collection of china inspired by the color scheme, and soon I had the opportunity to do so, for Lenox: a five-piece place-setting I titled Insignia. All the plates are different; they can stand alone or work in pairs, in trios, or all together. As the dinner progresses, each one tells a story, yet it also works in concert with all the components. The idea was to provide total versatility: With one set of china, we'd offer multiple options for people who like to entertain regularly. As soon as the collection was completed, Lenox shipped me a full set along with my new gold flatware. I was so excited opening the boxes that I immediately picked up the phone and started to invite a few friends for dinner that evening.

For the table arrangement, the goal was simple elegance. I avoided the standard solution—fresh-cut flowers—which would also have cost extra time and money. For the centerpiece, I brought a 1930s terra-cotta sculpture of a panther by André Vincent Becquerel down from the mantelpiece, framed it at either end with a pair of gilded porcelain obelisks, and flanked it with a wall of fire in the form of gold-leaf votive cups. I gathered these objects from around the house. The end result, albeit unintentional, was a somewhat formal presentation, with perhaps an Ancient Egyptian or Napoleonic theme. The obelisks lend the sculpture a ceremonious air; the votive candles give it dramatically flattering under-illumination. Instead of using placemats, runners, or a tablecloth, I anchored the place settings with big black chargers—part of my Insignia collection—that can also be used as dinner plates or serving plates (again, versatility being the key). The glasses and flatware were also my design from a previous collection and worked wonderfully.

THE MENU: SUPPER FOR SIX

 APPETIZER
FLOWER OF ENDIVE SALAD

MAIN COURSE
POT-ROASTED LOIN OF VEAL WITH
ARTICHOKES AND MUSHROOMS

DESSERT
CONFIT OF VANILLA-INFUSED PINEAPPLE
WITH VANILLA ICE CREAM

TO DRINK
COCKTAIL DE NUIT: VODKA MARTINI
WINE: A CHATEAUNEUF-DU-PAPE
SUCH AS CHATEAU BEAUCASTEL OR SOME OTHER FINE
RHONE-STYLE BLEND PROVIDES THE MEDIUM RICHNESS,
EARTHINESS, AND FIRM FINISH TO PAIR WITH
THE VEAL, ARTICHOKES, AND MUSHROOMS.

Since it was winter, we lit a fire and made the best of the warm, cozy atmosphere. It pays off to inject a touch of life into the room with some greenery—especially in the colder months. In this instance, I made a dramatic statement with some oversize monstera leaves, which are relatively inexpensive and last a long time. I really love the way they catch the light to warm the room.

On the table, I used amber water glasses, which I designed to reflect the silhouette of the wineglasses. Typically, I'll buy an antique set or choose a classic shape, updated. Then I'll acquire several more pieces to reflect that first shape, but with color or size variations. This way, with just two or three sets of glasses, you can easily create chic and elegant and soignée table settings.

TIMING The salad can be assembled in advance, then dressed immediately prior to serving. While we were enjoying the salad course, the pot-roasted veal—prepped and put in the oven before the guests arrived—was just finishing in the oven. The pineapple can be prepared a day in advance, stored in the fridge, and warmed prior to serving.

VODKA MARTINI

Our celebration started with a martini, the definitive cocktail—shaken, of course, not stirred. I like my martinis shaken hard at least 20 times so that the vodka gets very cold and you have little slivers of ice floating in the drink. This takes the sting out of it, making it go down more smoothly. The glasses should be chilled in advance by filling them with ice and cold water, which you pour out just before straining the vodka mixture into them; as an easier alternative, you can simply leave the glasses in the fridge for at least 30 minutes. The vodka is stored in the freezer. Everything about this drink is frosty, ice-cold, and sleek. As for garnishes, the classic martini takes a cocktail olive, either pitted and plain or pimiento-stuffed, depending on your preference. (The pimiento-stuffed have a bit sharper flavor.) There are also many types of gourmet olives; you can find them stuffed with chilies, almonds, garlic, and anchovies. Or you might choose cocktail onions or pickled tomatillos for your garnish. In any case, you must rinse the olives, onions, or any other pickled garnish well; otherwise, their pickling brine will float unattractively on the surface of the martinis.

12 OUNCES TOP-QUALITY VODKA (OR GIN)

1½–2 OUNCES DRY VERMOUTH
(OR LESS IF YOU PREFER IT "VERY DRY")

OLIVES OR LEMON PEEL, FOR GARNISH

1. Chill 6 martini glasses (see page 181).
2. Fill a shaker full of ice. Add the vodka (or gin) and vermouth. Shake well and strain into the glasses. Serve with olives or a twist.

Flower of Endive Salad

This first course is a foolproof salad I've served many times and it has never let me down. I love it because it has an aura of sensuality: In a dramatic moment at the table, you and your guests snip open up the endive flower to reveal the springy salad within. The recipe asks you to take a little extra time to arrange the presentation, but the payoff is tremendous. I'm always thoroughly in favor of any dish that looks as good as it tastes.

FOR THE SALAD

½ LEEK, WASHED THOROUGHLY
AND CUT LENGTHWISE INTO 1/4-INCH RIBBONS

SALT

1 BUNCH OF WATERCRESS,
TRIMMED, WASHED, AND DRIED

2 HEADS OF BABY FRISÉE LETTUCE,
TRIMMED, WASHED, AND DRIED

2 OUNCES CRUMBLED BLUE CHEESE (OR GOAT CHEESE)

1/4 CUP TOASTED PINE NUTS (SEE NOTE), CHOPPED

4 LARGE ENDIVES, WASHED (30 LEAVES)

½ BUNCH OF CHIVES, FINELY CHOPPED, FOR GARNISH

FOR THE VINAIGRETTE

1 TEASPOON DIJON MUSTARD

1 TEASPOON WHOLE-GRAIN MUSTARD

1/4 CUP RED WINE VINEGAR

1 TEASPOON COARSE SEA SALT, PLUS MORE TO TASTE

½ TEASPOON FRESHLY GROUND BLACK PEPPER,
PLUS MORE TO TASTE

3/4 CUP GRAPESEED OIL

1/4 CUP WALNUT OIL

1. Blanch the leek in a pot of boiling salted water for 1 minute (see Note). Plunge it into ice-cold water to stop the cooking. Set aside.

2. In a large mixing bowl, combine the watercress, baby frisée, cheese, and all but 1 tablespoon of the pine nuts.

3. To assemble each serving, select 6 endive leaves and place them upright in a tea cup, forming an open "flower" arrangement. Fill the inside of the flower with the salad mixture. Close the leaves together in the original shape of the endive and secure with a blanched leek ribbon. Trim the base of each flower so it can stand on its own. Repeat the process for each of the remaining

five portions. Set the salads aside (laying the flowers on their sides in a shallow dish) until you are ready to dress and serve them. They can be refrigerated for up to 2 hours. Cover with a damp paper towel and plastic wrap until ready to serve.

4. To make the vinaigrette, combine the mustards, vinegar, salt, and pepper in a mixing bowl. While whisking, slowly drizzle in the oils. Adjust the seasonings to taste. Set aside at room temperature for up to 30 minutes, or refrigerate if preparing well in advance.

5. To serve, place a single endive flower upright in the middle of each plate. Inject a small amount of the vinaigrette into each of the flowers with a squeeze bottle and drizzle some vinaigrette around the plate. Alternatively, you can serve the dressing in a gravy boat, pass it around, and let everyone dress his or her own salad. Garnish with the reserved tablespoon of chopped pine nuts and the chopped chives.

NOTE If you are working on your own, a loose rubber band can act as a second set of hands to help secure the bundles.

NOTE To toast pine nuts, simply place them in a cast-iron skillet over medium heat, shaking and turning them once or twice, until golden brown, 3 to 4 minutes. Alternatively, place them in a toaster oven, set to medium, and toast just until fragrant.

There are three principal types of endive, all members of the *Cichorium* family: Belgian endive, curly endive, and escarole. Belgian endive is the familiar, whitish oval-shaped leaf with pointed ends. Curly endive is its cousin, although it's often mislabeled chicory. Escarole is another form of curly endive. Belgian endive is grown in the dark so its leaves don't turn green. It's best served fresh but can be stored in the refrigerator for a few days wrapped in paper towel inside a sealed plastic bag. Chicory is a relative of endive; both frisée and radicchio are members of the chicory family.

Invest in a Salad Spinner

If you don't have one, run out and buy one immediately! It is really a must in terms of basic kitchen equipment, the only way to wash and dry your lettuces without brusing them. Otherwise, they stay wet, turn soggy, and dilute your dressing. Among kitchen implements, there is really no higher return on investment than the relatively small amount of money you'll spend on a good, reliable salad spinner.

PAN-ROASTED LOIN OF VEAL WITH ARTICHOKES AND MUSHROOMS

The main course is a classic one-pot meal: a boneless veal roast that features easy one-step preparation and doesn't require two or three hours of cooking. The veal loin is tender, elegant, and juicy, and is done in around an hour. In butcher's parlance, the cut of meat is a boned rack of veal. The same cut, with the bones left attached then separated in a cross section, yields six veal chops. There's no need to reduce the sauce in this dish. It's roasted covered, so as the meat cooks it steams and creates a delicious, savory juice. The pot vegetables—artichokes and mushrooms—form the side dish.

Roasted whole, on the bone, this cut is called rack of veal. Another good option is rack of lamb, which cooks in about 20 minutes instead of 40 to 45, depending on the size and the desired degree of doneness. (An internal temperature of 130° to 140°F. equals medium-rare for lamb.) Pork is another tasty option; it is a smaller cut as well, and it roasts in about 15 minutes after browning on the outside (internal temperature should be 145° to 150°F.).

6 LARGE ARTICHOKES, OUTER LEAVES REMOVED,
TIPS CUT AND CHOKES REMOVED

JUICE OF 1 LEMON

6 TABLESPOONS PLUS 1/2 CUP VEGETABLE OIL

1 4-POUND VEAL LOIN,
DEBONED AND TIED (HAVE YOUR BUTCHER DO THIS)

1 TABLESPOON PLUS 1 TEASPOON COARSE SEA SALT

1 TABLESPOON PLUS 1 TEASPOON FRESHLY GROUND
BLACK PEPPER

2 TABLESPOONS OLIVE OIL

24 PEARL ONIONS

1/2 POUND EACH OF PORTOBELLO AND
SHIITAKE MUSHROOMS, CLEANED AND COARSELY SLICED

1 TABLESPOON CRUSHED GARLIC

1 BUNCH (12 TO 18 LEAVES) OF FRESH SAGE,
1 TABLESPOON CHOPPED, BALANCE RESERVED WHOLE

2 CUPS VEAL STOCK (PAGE 186)

1 TABLESPOON CHOPPED FRESH FLAT-LEAF PARSLEY

1. Preheat the oven to 350°F.

2. Cut off the top two thirds of the artichokes and then cut them into quarters. Using a paring knife, trim off the hard, stringy outer parts. Trim the stems to a length of 1 inch. Separate the leaves and, using a teaspoon, scoop out the choke. Place the trimmed artichoke quarters and the lemon juice in a 1- to 2-quart mixing bowl full of water. Set aside.

3. Place 2 tablespoons of the vegetable oil in a large pot over

(continued on page 18)

911

Canned artichoke hearts work just as well in a stew or roast as the peeled and prepped fresh ones—as long as they're not pickled. They shouldn't be added to the pot until 5 to 10 minutes before serving.

medium-low heat. Season the veal all over with 1 tablespoon each of the salt and pepper. Place in the pot and cook, turning, until brown all over, about 2 minutes per side. Remove the veal and set aside. Remove the excess fat from the pot. Drain the water from the bowl of artichokes, add the 2 tablespoons of olive oil, the remaining 1 teaspoon each of salt and pepper, and toss well.

4. Add 2 tablespoons of vegetable oil to the pot, then add the artichokes, onions, and mushrooms and sauté for 5 minutes. Add the chopped garlic, chopped sage, and stock. Return the veal to the pot, cover, and place it in the oven to roast for 1 hour, or until tender. (It takes about 10 minutes per pound for medium-rare; the internal temperature should be 125°F. for medium-rare to 140°F. for medium.)

5. Remove the artichokes, mushrooms, and veal from the pot and arrange on a large serving dish or platter. Allow the roast to stand for 15 to 20 minutes before slicing and serving. Skim the excess fat from the pot with a wide spoon or soup ladle, and serve the cooking juices along with the meat and vegetables.

6. While the roast is resting, prepare the crispy fried-sage garnish (see Note): Heat the ½ cup of vegetable oil in a small skillet over medium-high heat. When the oil is hot but not smoking, place the reserved whole sage in the skillet in a single layer and fry briefly until crispy, about 10 seconds. (Make sure you fry it in light oil that is very hot. If not, the sage will just soak up the oil and get soggy. To test whether the oil is ready for frying, drop a small torn-off piece of sage leaf into it; if the leaf sizzles, the oil is ready.) Drain the fried sage on a paper towel. Arrange the sage on top of the roast, sprinkle chopped parsley around the platter, and serve.

NOTE The versatile fried-sage garnish can also be used with a grilled or pan-seared steak.

Confit of Vanilla-Infused Pineapple with Vanilla Ice Cream

It's quite a fancy-sounding dish and fairly spectacular to serve, but it's really quite simple to prepare. I often collaborate with Martin Herold, a friend and gifted chef from Alsace who now lives in the United States. It's infrequent that you encounter vanilla and pineapple in the same equation; it was Martin's idea to combine this tropical fruit (pineapple) with this tropical pod (the vanilla bean) so uniquely. The finished recipe provides a delightful element of contrast between the warmth of the pineapple and the coolness of the vanilla ice cream.

The best pineapples in my opinion are the Del Monte Golds. Their interiors should be a warm yellowish-gold color. Any pineapple that is whitish on the interior is going to be too sour.

1 RIPE PINEAPPLE,
TOUGH OUTER SKIN CUT OFF WITH A SHARP KNIFE

4 VANILLA BEANS,
CUT IN HALF ALONG THE HORIZONTAL AXIS AND THEN CUT
IN HALF ALONG THE VERTICAL (16 PIECES TOTAL)

4 CUPS BROWN SUGAR

2 CUPS DARK RUM

1 PINT VANILLA ICE CREAM

1. Use a wooden skewer or large toothpick to poke holes from the exterior toward the center of the pineapple. Insert the slivers of vanilla beans into the holes.

2. Place the pineapple in a deep roasting pan and add 8 cups of water or enough to completely cover the fruit. Add the sugar and rum, and bring the liquid to a boil over high heat. Reduce the heat to medium low, and simmer for 1 hour. The recipe can be prepared to this point in advance; in that case, the pineapple should be placed in a container or bowl, covered with its juice, and then refrigerated until ready to be served, either warmed up or at room temperature.

3. To serve, remove the pot from the stove and allow the pineapple to cool in its own syrup. Slice and serve while still slightly warm, drizzled with syrup and with a scoop of vanilla ice cream on the side.

411: Confit

A traditional *confit* is the ancient specialty of Gascogne (or Gascogny) and surrounding areas of southwestern France. Meats such as goose, duck, pork, or turkey are preserved by salting them, slowly cooking them in their own fat, and then packing them in the fat to be stored away. A similar method is applied here to the pineapple, which cooks slowly in the sugar syrup, infusing the fruit with tropical flavor.

A Lighter Touch

A summer option, to make the dish even more tropical, is to substitute mango or passion-fruit sorbet for the vanilla ice cream.

911

If you don't have the time to prepare the pineapple from scratch, fry or sauté slices of pineapple in a pan with butter, brown sugar, and a dash of vanilla extract. Deglaze the pan with rum and serve with a scoop of ice cream.

Fashion Week, NYC
for 6

Fashion Week is an exciting time in New York City. The designers' new collections are being presented at shows all over town. The entire island of Manhattan is abuzz. The glitterati of the haute couture, ready-to-wear, and retail worlds—the arbiters of style and taste—are coming and going. Everybody's looking over his or her shoulder for the latest trend, what's in and what's out, what's hot and what's not. There is plenty of talk, from serious exchanges of information and ideas to just plain juicy gossip. All of it is tremendous fun. Cha! Cha! Cha!

There are two fashion weeks each year. We held our dinner during the one in April, when the upcoming fall collections are being shown; there's another one in September for the spring collections.

Our hostess for this evening was my dear friend Kalliope Karella, who has a splendid Upper East Side apartment decorated by the designer Robert Couturier. It's full of fine antiques, tapestries, and an impressive collection of art. The decor has a warm, rich feel—bold and opulent yet tasteful and comfortable. Among the guests was the eminently fashionable hairdressing mogul Frédéric Fekkai.

Since I'm a devotee of Italian designers, I decided to create a menu with an Italian accent. We started with the natural choice, pasta, and came up with a colorful, appetizing, and easy-to-prepare dish. In the spirit of unveiling a beautiful surprise, the main course was wild sea bass baked in a crust of sea salt. The dessert comes under the intriguing name of sgroppino and is quintessentially Italian, exciting and fashionable.

The centerpiece for the table was both easy and elegant—the epitome of the kind of installation I try to create for most occasions. It gets accolades while demanding a minimal amount of time and trouble. I used a very large glass bowl with a Greek key pattern etched and gilded around its edge to create a shallow lagoon, in which I floated candles and a few really spectacular specimen peonies. These are big, bold, and beautiful, and they float ever-so-gracefully in the pond. It's cosmic: Of the four classical elements, you've got earth, fire, and water. All you're missing is air, and with luck there will be a glowing sunset out the window to complete the picture.

LIGHTING

Rule number one: Every light switch in the house should have a dimmer. They are convenient, readily available, and inexpensive, and they do so much to transform the ambience of any setting. After a long day at work, the first thing you want to do is dim the lights. It's so much more soothing and relaxing. A principle I've learned from designing large parties and special events: What you don't light, no one sees, and what you do light jumps out at you.

A few more helpful hints about lighting:

• Try placing lights in different or interesting places, for example under the table or behind a plant. Under-lighting gives a wonderfully dramatic effect.

• Avoid fluorescent lights at all costs. They flicker and their harsh white light is never flattering. Instead, use soft-light bulbs—such as pink or light amber—wherever possible.

"DRESSING" THE TABLE

Entertaining, like dressing, is a form of personal expression. We've all mastered the art of dressing ourselves, of making a unique personal statement through the clothes we choose to wear. The next arena in which we can express our sense of style is the table. Whenever I go about devising table arrangements and decorations, I try to think both visually and graphically. My notion is to bring a fashion sensibility to the dining room, to "dress up the table" just as a fashion designer dresses models for a runway show.

THE MENU: SUPPER FOR SIX

ADPETIZER
PASTA TRICOLORE

MAIN COURSE
SALT-CRUSTED WILD STRIPED BASS WITH
BRAISED FENNEL AND GARLIC AÏOLI

DESSERT
SGROPPINO WITH CHERRIES
"CIGARETTE" COOKIES

TO DRINK
COCKTAILS DE NUIT: A CHOICE OF CAMPARI AND
SODA OR CAMPARI AND GRAPEFRUIT JUICE
WINE: ITALIAN WHITE
SILVIO JERMANN'S SUPERB FRIULIAN BLEND "DREAMS"
WOULD BE AN EXCELLENT CHOICE, AS WOULD HIS
"VINTAGE TUNINA," A MASTERFUL BLEND OF CHARDONNAY,
SAUVIGNON BLANC, AND AS MANY AS FIVE OTHER LESSER-KNOWN
GRAPES. MANY CONSIDER IT ITALY'S BEST WHITE WINE.

TIMING The pasta takes 15 to 20 minutes and needs to be served immediately while still hot; if you have everything ready, you can cook it quickly at the end of the cocktail hour. The fish takes 1 hour to bake; it should be prepared ahead and put in the oven as soon as the guests arrive. The fennel takes about an hour and can be made ahead and kept warm in the oven. The garlic aïoli should be made in advance, refrigerated, and taken out of the fridge shortly before serving. The sgroppino takes just a few minutes to assemble and prepare and can also be done à *la minute.* The cookies can be baked in advance or brought from the store.

COCKTAILS DE NUIT

It's nice to have a choice when it comes to cocktails. In this case, we offered two variations based on the bright red–colored Italian bitter apéritif Campari. We also had a couple of bottles of vintage Bollinger Champagne, well chilled, for those who preferred the bubbly. (Our hostess, the lovely Kalliope, thoroughly enjoyed this option.)

CAMPARI AND SODA OR CAMPARI AND GRAPEFRUIT JUICE

Fill each highball glass with ice and add 2 ounces of Campari. Top each glass off with sparkling water or club soda, garnish with a thin slice of lemon and/or orange, and serve.

For the grapefruit option: Fill a rocks or highball glass with ice, add 2 ounces of Campari, top off with pink grapefruit juice, and garnish with a slice of orange.

PASTA TRICOLORE

This is a festive, colorful, tasty pasta dish that, in keeping with our fashion theme, looks as good as it tastes. With its red, green, and white ingredients (tomato, basil, and cheese), it displays the three colors of the Italian flag, affectionately referred to as the *tricolore*. So why not call it Pasta Tricolore? Feel free to experiment with this recipe; for example, leave out the tomato sauce, use sausage instead of the ham, and use broccoli rabe instead of the radicchio.

1 POUND LINGUINI

1 TABLESPOON EXTRA-VIRGIN OLIVE OIL

1/4 POUND IMPORTED SMOKED HAM (SPECK
OR BLACK FOREST), FAT TRIMMED AND CUT INTO 1/4-INCH CUBES

1 SMALL WHITE ONION, DICED

1 HEAD OF RADICCHIO, CORED AND COARSELY CHOPPED

2 CUPS TOMATO SAUCE (RECIPE FOLLOWS)

1/2 CUP FRESH BASIL LEAVES,
TORN INTO SMALL STRIPS BY HAND

1/2 POUND SMOKED MOZZARELLA,
CUT INTO 1/2-INCH CUBES

1/2 CUP FRESHLY GRATED TUSCAN PECORINO OR
PARMIGIANO-REGGIANO CHEESE

COARSE SEA SALT AND FRESHLY GROUND
BLACK PEPPER, TO TASTE

1. Cook the pasta al dente according to the instructions on the box. Drain and reserve 1 cup of the cooking water.
2. While the pasta is cooking, place the olive oil in a large skillet over medium heat. (Make sure the skillet is large enough to hold the sauce and the pasta.) Add the ham and onions and sauté for 8 to 10 minutes, until the onions are soft and golden.
3. Add the radicchio and stir until wilted, about 1 minute. Add the tomato sauce and the drained pasta, and continue to cook, stirring, for 2 minutes. Add the basil, mozzarella, and grated cheese, season with salt and pepper, mix well, and serve. If necessary, thin the sauce with a few tablespoons of the cooking water from the pasta.

TOMATO SAUCE

2 TABLESPOONS OLIVE OIL

1 MEDIUM YELLOW ONION, CHOPPED (ABOUT 1 CUP)

1 GARLIC CLOVE, MINCED

1 28-OUNCE CAN PEELED TOMATOES WITH BASIL

1 TABLESPOON CHOPPED FRESH BASIL LEAVES
OR DRIED BASIL

1 TEASPOON SALT

1/2 TEASPOON FRESHLY GROUND BLACK PEPPER

1 TEASPOON SUGAR

1. Place the oil in a large saucepan over medium-high heat. Add the onion and sauté, stirring frequently, until soft and translucent, about 5 minutes. Add the garlic and sauté for 3 minutes.
2. Purée the tomatoes in a blender or food processor until smooth. Add to the pan and allow the mixture to come to a boil. Season with the basil, salt, pepper, and sugar. Reduce the heat and simmer for about 15 minutes, skimming off any surface foam with a large cooking spoon.

Salt-Crusted Wild Striped Bass with Braised Fennel and Garlic Aïoli

Here's a dish guaranteed to elicit a few ooh's and aah's from your guests as you carefully crack open the crust to reveal the steaming, fragrant fish within. In Italy, they call these magnificent creatures *branzino;* in New England and on the East Coast of America, they're known by the less mellifluous name *striped bass.*

¾ CUP FAVA BEANS, OUTER SKINS REMOVED

1 TEASPOON PLUS 2 TABLESPOONS OLIVE OIL

SEA SALT AND FRESHLY GROUND BLACK PEPPER TO TASTE

GREENS (LEAVES) OF 6 MEDIUM FENNEL BULBS
(RESERVED FROM BRAISED FENNEL; RECIPE FOLLOWS)

1 8-POUND WILD STRIPED BASS (SEE NOTE),
CLEANED, GUTTED, AND SCALED, HEAD ON

4 POUNDS KOSHER SALT

12 LARGE EGG WHITES

2 LEMONS, CUT INTO WEDGES, FOR GARNISH

GARLIC AÏOLI (PAGE 106)

1. Preheat the oven to 400°F.
2. Bring a large pot of salted water to a rolling boil. Add the beans and cook for 1 minute. Drain and remove hard shells. Toss with 1 teaspoon of the olive oil, season to taste with salt and pepper, and set aside.
3. Place a third of the fennel leaves inside the cavity of the fish.
4. In a large mixing bowl, combine the salt and egg whites with ¾ cup water. Stir until a compact dough is formed, the consistency of a sand castle so it can be molded. If the dough is runny, add salt as needed; if too thick, add water.
5. Coat the fish with the remaining 2 tablespoons olive oil. Take a third of the dough and spread it evenly, patting it down by hand, onto a baking sheet large enough to hold the fish. Form a depression to fit the size and shape of the fish. Lay a third of the fennel greens on top. Place the fish on the dough bed and cover it with the remaining greens. Spread the balance of the dough on top of the fish to blanket it entirely. Mold and press the dough to fit the shape of the fish snugly.
6. Bake the fish for 1 hour (10 to 12 minutes per pound).
7. Remove the fish from the oven. Crack the crust around the sides with a small hammer or the handle of a large kitchen knife, and lift the top using the blade of the knife. Discard the crust.

Remove the fennel leaves and discard. Some of the fish's skin will come off with the crust; clean the rest of the skin and excess salt gently by scraping with the side of a knife, a serving spoon, or a spatula. Garnish the fish with lemon wedges and serve with the braised fennel and garlic aïoli on the side.

NOTE This recipe can also be prepared using red snapper. If the fish is too large to fit on the baking tray, remove the head and/or tail. Unless you plan on catching it yourself, you should order a large striped bass in advance from your fishmonger. Otherwise, you can substitute farm-raised 1-pound striped bass, which are available year round and can each be encrusted in their own salt dough and presented individually at the table. In this case, be sure to provide guests with a way of cracking open the salt crusts, and also provide a large bowl or dish for the discarded items. The salt crust should not be placed on the fish more than 45 minutes before baking.

BRAISED FENNEL

3 MEDIUM FENNEL BULBS,
TOPS REMOVED AND RESERVED, OUTER LAYER REMOVED,
CUT LENGTHWISE INTO 6 WEDGES EACH

4 TABLESPOONS OLIVE OIL

1 MEDIUM WHITE ONION, THINLY SLICED

2 GARLIC CLOVES, PEELED AND SLICED

2 BAY LEAVES

1 CUP CHICKEN STOCK (PAGE 120)

1 TEASPOON COARSE SEA SALT

½ TEASPOON FRESHLY GROUND BLACK PEPPER

1. Preheat the oven to 350°F.
2. Chop enough of the reserved fennel greens to yield 1 to 2 tablespoons, for garnish. Use the remaining greens for the fish.
3. Heat the oil over medium flame in an ovenproof sauté pan or shallow braising pan large enough to hold all the fennel. Add the fennel and onion, and sauté for approximately 5 minutes, or until lightly brown. Add the garlic, bay leaves, and chicken stock. Season with salt and pepper. Bring to a boil, cover, and place in the oven for 40 to 50 minutes, until the fennel is tender.
4. To serve, arrange the fennel on a platter, pour the remaining liquid on top, and garnish with the chopped fennel greens.

411: Prosecco

Prosecco is a light, dry, sparkling white wine produced in the Veneto (the province of Italy around Venice) and traditionally consumed as an apéritif. It's often thought of as a kind of poor man's Champagne, but many connoisseurs consider it to be among the very best of sparklers. The finer appellation-controlled, or DOC, Proseccos are labeled "Prosecco di Conegliano-Valdobbiadene." Sweeter versions have a lovely fruit bouquet and taste, while the drier ones are slightly bitter. The highest-quality Proseccos come under the designation Superiore di Cartizze.

SGROPPINO WITH CHERRIES

The Hotel Cipriani in Venice is one of the premier hotels in all of Europe, and this is a cocktail I discovered there—and enjoy regularly. It travels quite well, and in my opinion it works even better as a dessert than as an apéritif.

1 PINT LEMON SORBET,
SOFTENED AT ROOM TEMPERATURE FOR 5 TO 10 MINUTES

4 OUNCES VODKA

10 OUNCES PROSECCO
(ITALIAN SPARKLING WINE), CHILLED

1 POUND FRESH CHERRIES

Whisk the sorbet, vodka, and Prosecco together in a bowl until creamy and thick. Serve immediately in a champagne flute with "Cigarette" Cookies (recipe follows) and some cherries, when in season; they're sexy and alive, and they lend a beautiful touch.

"Cigarette" Cookies

This is a variation of the traditional tuile, which is a thin cookie bent into a crescent shape over a rolling pin while still warm. It's a wonderfully simple recipe yielding cookies with a delightful sweetness, texture, and mouth-feel—not to mention their artful shape.

Makes 12 cookies

¼ cup unsalted butter, softened
1 cup confectioners' sugar
2 medium egg whites
½ cup all-purpose flour, sifted
½ teaspoon vanilla extract

1. In a large mixing bowl, use a wooden spoon to combine the butter and sugar. Stir until well incorporated. Add the egg whites one by one, stirring well each time. Add the flour and vanilla extract, and mix well. Cover the bowl and place it in the refrigerator for 1 hour.

2. Preheat the oven to 350°F.

3. Line two nonstick baking pans or insulated cookie sheets with parchment paper. Lay 6 thin disks of dough, about 4 inches in diameter, onto each of the sheets. Use a spatula to make flat, evenly shaped rectangles. Bake for 3 to 4 minutes, until light golden.

4. Remove the cookies from the oven. While they are still warm, carefully lift them from the parchment paper and roll them into cylinders either by hand or by briefly draping over the handle of a wooden spoon (remove almost immediately) before serving.

Place Cards

I'm a firm believer in providing seating placements for my guests—whenever and wherever appropriate. (Professionally, we always do it for large formal occasions, but sometimes it's called for with smaller parties.) The reason? First, putting guests in a pre-determined spot allows me to account for the yin and yang of various personalities, to ensure social equilibrium, and to balance the energy at the table. If I know Jane's a live wire and Mary's one, too, I'll put them at opposite ends; if I seat them side by side, the other half of the table is going to be dead by comparison. I always try to alternate boy-girl around the table as well as to separate best friends, and husbands and wives. (They see enough of each other.) Another practical aspect of place cards: They're a valuable crutch for those who might have a difficult time remembering names.

OTT

If you want to take the red theme to the max, screw in a red lightbulb near your front door.

Since the apartment is so impeccably decorated, I didn't feel the need for flowers on the dinner table. In keeping with our red theme, I used the ample space at the center of this large square table to create an installation of tomatoes and peppers, which I encircled with an honor guard of votive candles in their red cups.

A tomato isn't just a tomato anymore: It's an art form. There are literally dozens of varieties, a good number of which are available in just about any grocery store—cherry tomatoes, plums, Romas, vine-ripened, and so forth. Use this multiplicity to your advantage to create an eye-catching assemblage. Add some bright red peppers for contrast. Instead of place cards, for an amusing flourish, I laid a red pepper on each charger plate and labeled it with a guest's name using a Magic Marker.

TIMING The Zurra cocktail requires a few minutes of advance preparation for the sugar-mint syrup. The Peri-Peri Prawns need to marinate for several hours, so prepare them in advance; their actual cooking time is very brief. The dessert can be made in advance and should chill in the fridge for at least an hour, so it, too, should be prepared in advance of the guests' arrival. The chicken livers take 15 to 20 minutes, including prep time; they must be served hot, so cook them at the end of cocktail hour, and seat your guests just before presenting the livers. You're in for a spicy night!

The Menu: Supper for Eight

Appetizer
Spicy Portuguese Chicken Livers

Main Course
Peri-Peri Prawns with Garlic-Lemon Butter
Portuguese Rice

Dessert
Strawberry Soup with Champagne and Mint

To Drink
Cocktail de Nuit: Zurra or Champagne
Wine: Domaine Ott
A wonderful rosé from Provence, with the dinner,
or Mulderbosch Rosé from South Africa

Zurra

Zurra—what an intriguing, exotic name. It's a refreshing, sophisti-cated wine cooler, like a Portuguese version of sangría, but with white wine rather than red.

1/2 CUP SUGAR
1 1/2 CUPS WATER
1 BUNCH OF FRESH MINT LEAVES
4 CINNAMON STICKS
2 LEMONS, SLICED INTO SECTIONS
2 BLOOD ORANGES, SLICED
(A REGULAR ORANGE CAN BE SUBSTITUTED)
2 PEACHES, SLICED
1 (750-MILLILITER) BOTTLE CHILLED DRY WHITE WINE
1 (16-OUNCE) BOTTLE OF SPARKLING WATER
OR CLUB SODA

1. Combine the sugar, water, and half of the mint in a small saucepan. Bring the liquid to a boil and simmer for 5 minutes over medium heat. Set aside to cool to room temperature.
2. Place the cinnamon along with the lemon, orange, and peach slices in a large pitcher or jug. Add the wine, then the sugar mixture. Stir well, pour into glasses over ice, top each glass with 2 ounces of sparkling water or club soda, garnish with mint leaves, and serve.

SPICY PORTUGUESE CHICKEN LIVERS

This dish is rich, gratifying, and easy to make. I find a dense food like chicken livers benefits enormously from a lively, spicy preparation like this one. I highly recommend serving the livers with a rustic, peasant-style bread so you can soak up their generous mouthwatering sauce.

4 MEDIUM YELLOW ONIONS, DICED

1/4 POUND BACON, DICED
(PANCETTA CAN BE SUBSTITUTED)

4 MEDIUM TOMATOES, PEELED
(SEE PAGE 57), SEEDED, AND DICED

2 TEASPOONS COARSE SEA SALT, PLUS MORE TO TASTE

1 TEASPOON FRESHLY GROUND BLACK PEPPER,
PLUS MORE TO TASTE

1/2 TEASPOON SUGAR

4 TABLESPOONS VEGETABLE OIL

2 POUNDS CHICKEN LIVERS, CLEANED

2 TEASPOONS DRIED HOT RED CHILI FLAKES

2 TABLESPOONS FINELY CHOPPED FLAT-LEAF PARSLEY

JUICE OF 2 LIMES

1. Place the onions and bacon in a medium skillet over medium heat. Cook for 10 minutes, until brown, then remove from the heat. Add the tomatoes to the skillet, season to taste with the salt, pepper, and sugar, stir well, and set aside.

2. Place the vegetable oil in a frying pan large enough to hold all the chicken livers in one layer over medium-high heat. Season the livers with 2 teaspoons salt and 1 teaspoon pepper. When the oil in the pan begins to smoke, add the livers and the chili flakes. Sear the livers on both sides until brown, approximately 1 minute per side. Add the bacon-onion-tomato mixture to the pan, stir well, and continue cooking for an additional 2 minutes. Add the parsley and lime juice, remove from the heat, season with additional salt and pepper to taste, and serve hot with sliced baquettes on the side to soak up the pan juices.

Wines to Pair with Spicy Foods
One of my top sources for wine knowledge is Christian Navarro at Wally's Wines and Spirits in Los Angeles. Christian and I discussed the challenge of pairing wines with spicy foods. The key is to find wines that possess sufficient fruitiness and body, richness and flavor to stand up to the heat. Wine professionals use a technical term, residual sugar, to refer to the fructose that survives alcoholic fermentation in some wines. But that term can be somewhat misleading. Wines containing residual sugar aren't necessarily sweet in a "desktop" sense, but rather they feature a light, essential natural sweetness, at a nearly undetectable level, that puts out the fire of the spicier Indian and Asian dishes. It's akin to biting into a fresh peach as opposed to eating a peach cobbler.

The first wines that come to mind in pairing with spicy foods are the Alsatians: Pinot Gris, Gewürztraminer, and Riesling. German Riesling Spätleses, which are a cut above the simpler, drier Kabinetts in fruitiness, would also be a good pairing, but not the sweeter Ausleses, which might have too much sugar and body. Among other white wines, the Vouvray *demi-secs*—not the bone-dry *secs* nor the sweeter late-harvest *moelleux* —made from the Chenin Blanc grapes, work well with Asian spices, as do the Savennières. Try the California versions of these wines as well.

Among red wines, successful pairings with spicy foods can be tough to find. But a shiraz from the Southern Hemisphere—primarily Australia—is bright, fruity, and intense enough to stand up to the fire. Spanish Tempranillos have a lot of new oak and pizzaz as well. California zinfandels and petite syrahs will also work.

Peri-Peri Prawns with Garlic-Lemon Butter

These prawns, cooked under the broiler and basted with a hot sauce, are one of my all-time favorite seafood recipes. I always like to offer some garlic-butter sauce to pass around the table. And the dish is never right without its sidekick, Portuguese Rice. The combination of the rice, chili, butter sauces, and shrimp will certainly take you on a memorable journey. And you have my license to suck and chew on the shells—that's where some of the best flavor comes from.

32 JUMBO PRAWNS (MINIMUM SIZE: 12 PER POUND)
4 HOT RED OR GREEN
(JALAPEÑO OR SIMILAR) CHILI PEPPERS, COARSELY CHOPPED
4 TABLESPOONS FINELY CHOPPED GARLIC
JUICE OF 2 LEMONS
8 TABLESPOONS OLIVE OIL
1 TEASPOON CHOPPED FRESH FLAT-LEAF PARSLEY
1 TEASPOON CHOPPED FRESH CILANTRO
GARLIC-LEMON BUTTER (RECIPE FOLLOWS)

1. Butterfly the prawns: Using a sharp, pointed knife, make an incision the length of the underside of the shell. Cut through the underside of the shell, almost all the way through the flesh. Spread the prawn flat. If the cutting exposes a dark vein, pull it out using the knife or your fingers. Be sure to leave the shell on; it will keep the flesh moist and succulent. (Alternatively, have your fishmonger butterfly them for you.)
2. In a food processor, combine the chopped chili peppers, garlic, lemon juice, olive oil, parsley, and cilantro. Pulse until the ingredients form a smooth paste. Place the prawns in a glass dish, rub them all over with the paste, mix well, cover with plastic wrap, and refrigerate for 2 to 3 hours.
3. Preheat the broiler.
4. Lay the shrimp in a single layer on a foil-lined baking pan (see Note), flesh side down. Broil for 1 minute. Turn the shrimp flesh side up and broil for 1 additional minute.
5. Meanwhile, prepare the garlic-lemon butter. Transfer it to individual bowls and serve alongside the prawns for dipping.
6. After the main course, it's thoughtful to bring out some chilled damp towels for everyone to wipe off their hands properly. The towels can be scented with lemon or rosewater.

NOTE The prawns can be grilled on a barbecue by placing them in a fish basket, and cooking 1 minute per side.

Garlic-Lemon Butter

1 STICK (1/2 CUP) UNSALTED BUTTER,
AT ROOM TEMPERATURE
2 GARLIC CLOVES, FINELY MINCED
JUICE OF 1 LEMON
1/2 TEASPOON SALT
1/4 TEASPOON WHITE PEPPER

Place the butter and garlic in a medium saucepan over medium heat. Melt the butter, whisking constantly, then add the lemon juice. If the garlic begins to sizzle, lower the heat so that it doesn't turn brown and bitter. When the butter is melted and the garlic has softened, after about 2 minutes, add the salt and pepper, then remove from the heat, stir to mix well, and serve immediately.

PORTUGUESE RICE

This is an all-purpose rice that can be prepared quickly and easily —and in advance—using a rice cooker. It's full of flavor, with a sweetness from the raisins to balance the spice of our main dishes.

2 TABLESPOONS UNSALTED BUTTER
1 MEDIUM YELLOW ONION, CHOPPED (ABOUT 1/2 CUP)
1 TEASPOON GROUND TURMERIC
2 CUPS WHITE BASMATI RICE, WASHED AND WELL RINSED
3 CUPS CHICKEN STOCK (PAGE 120)
1/2 CUP GOLDEN RAISINS
1/2 CUP DARK RAISINS
2 CINNAMON STICKS
1 TABLESPOON COARSE SEA SALT

1. Melt the butter in a large skillet over medium heat. Reduce the heat to low, add the onion and turmeric, and cook uncovered for 10 minutes, or until the onion is soft. Add the rice, stock, raisins, cinnamon, and salt. Bring to a boil, reduce the heat to low, cover, and cook for 20 minutes, or until all the liquid is absorbed.
2. Remove from the heat and keep covered for 5 minutes. Fluff with a fork, discard the cinnamon, transfer to a platter, and serve.

STRAWBERRY SOUP WITH CHAMPAGNE AND MINT

You might call this a *coulis,* which is the term for a purée of fruit and sugar. But I've added the fresh quartered strawberries, champagne, and sorbet, transforming it into a full-fledged soup. What I love about this dessert is it's really just a simple blend of several basic ingredients. Yet what could be more elegant than a strawberry soup with champagne? It's also a tremendously welcome refresher after a tantalizingly spicy meal.

2 CUPS UNSWEETENED FROZEN STRAWBERRIES,
THAWED (SEE NOTE)
1 CUP SUGAR
1 TABLESPOON LEMON JUICE
2 POUNDS FRESH STRAWBERRIES, CLEANED AND HULLED
4 TABLESPOONS FINELY SLICED MINT
2 PINTS LIME SORBET
2 CUPS (1/2 BOTTLE) CHAMPAGNE

1. In a blender, purée the frozen strawberries. Pass through a sieve into a large mixing bowl to remove the seeds. Add the sugar and lemon juice and mix well.
2. Cut the fresh strawberries into quarters, add to the bowl, and mix well. Stir in the mint, then place the bowl in the refrigerator for at least 1 hour prior to serving.
3. To serve, divide the berry mixture evenly among 8 serving bowls. Add a scoop of the lime sorbet to each bowl, and top each with chilled champagne at the table.

NOTE As an alternative, you could use ripe fresh strawberries to make the purée. Simply wash and trim, then pass the strawberries through a food mill, and proceed with the recipe.

Cuba Libre!
for 12

In life, we always want what we can't have. These days, Cuba is the forbidden fruit, which of course makes it taste all that much better. If you can't go to Cuba, why not bring Cuba to you? This is exactly what we did for a lively summer cocktail party at the home of my friend the adorable Lulu de Kwiatkowski, who is a very talented designer of fabrics and table linens.

The menu is designed as a "heavy hors d'oeuvres supper." After a cocktail party like this, you won't need dinner. You can go out dancing all night and mambo until you drop! Be sure to let your guests know in advance that it's not a sit-down dinner, but that there will be plenty of food served along with tasty libations.

We set up a bar with an assorted bunch of oversized mismatched glasses that I've collected over the years. I've found them in flea markets, at garage sales, at department-store clearances, you name it. I must have at least one hundred of them, although I rarely assemble this many at once. It's one of those whimsical items that you can really have some fun with once you've amassed a considerable collection. Each guest was given the opportunity to pick a favorite glass and have it filled with his or her drink of choice—a Cuba Libre, a Mojito, chilled beer, or Spanish wine. As the host, I usually like to start out mixing the drinks, but I'm always amenable to letting others take over. It gives people a good feeling of participation. The drinks station was fully stocked with buckets of ice to hold all the drinks. The setup was complete and self-contained, so if the bartender disappeared for a moment, any thirsty guests could quite easily help themselves.

The food was presented in wave after wave of large flat baskets, which functioned as serving trays. We began with the escabeche and ended with the fried bananas for "dessert." The focal point of the table was one big lovely bunch of green bananas and lots of red votive candles. In my continuing quest to avoid cut flowers, I featured extra-large tropical leaves. They lined the food-service baskets and were also arranged in vases around the apartment. Lulu's remarkable leaf-print fabrics provided an ideal backdrop to the tropical look.

HORS D'OEUVRES
ESCABECHE OF SWORDFISH
PICADILLO IN A LETTUCE CUP WITH
FRESH TOMATO SALSA
FRESHLY FRIED TORTILLAS
PLANTAIN CHIPS
COLIN'S CUBAN SANDWICHES
ARROZ CON CAMARONES

DESSERT
FRIED BANANAS WITH CARAMEL SAUCE

TO DRINK
COCKTAILS DE NUIT: MOJITO AND CUBA LIBRE
ADDITIONAL CHOICES: BEER, WHITE WINE, COCA-COLA,
SPARKLING WATER, ASSORTED FRUIT JUICES AND SODAS

TIMING The escabeche needs to marinate for a minimum of 8 hours, so it should be made at least the morning of the party if not a day or two in advance. The salsa can also be made in advance. The grilled cheese sandwiches need to be served immediately, hot. The plantain chips can be kept crispy in the oven on the lowest setting (150–200°F.). The shrimp and rice dish can be made ahead and kept warm in the oven as well. The picadillo of ground beef can be made before the guests arrive and reheated in the pan briefly to be served warm.

MUSIC Start with Cachao, Buena Vista Social Club, and Los Van Van, and branch out from there. I'd also highly recommend the CDs of Africando, a group of Cuban musicians backing an all-star lineup of African singers. Try to find somebody who's an expert on Latin music, tell them which artists and sounds you like, and ask them to steer you. Buy some of the solo albums from the artists on the Buena Vista Social Club roster. Investigate Cachao, a bassist and bandleader in the late forties and early fifties, whose real name was Israel López; he is considered one of the greatest practitioners of original-style mambo. When it comes to classic Cuban sounds, his music may be the epitome.

MOJITO

If there's one drink associated with the romance of mid-twentieth-century Cuba, the era when Hemingway helped us all discover its incredible allure, this is it. The authentic Mojito is made with light rum, but it can also be made with vodka.

1 ½ TO 2 OUNCES SIMPLE SYRUP (SEE 411)
1 ½ TO 2 OUNCES FRESH LIME JUICE
1 ½ TO 2 OUNCES LIGHT RUM
1 SPRIG OF FRESH MINT LEAVES

Fill a rocks glass (or small highball) with ice and add the rest of the ingredients, including the mint. Stir, lightly crushing the mint leaves into the ice cubes, and serve.

CUBA LIBRE

Cuba Libres can be made with light rum, but most people prefer a good-quality dark rum. They can also be made at varying strengths —anywhere from a single shot of liquor to half a glass. Be sure to ask your guest's preference.

To make a Cuba Libre, fill a highball glass with ice. Add 1½ ounces (or more) of rum and top off the glass with Coca-Cola. Garnish with a wedge of lemon.

Escabeche of Swordfish

Swordfish has a dense texture that has a tendency to go dry when it's cooked. For this reason, one of the best ways to prepare it is to cut it into cubes, then marinate and cook the cubes as brochettes. In this case, the fish is browned briefly and *then* marinated for up to several days. It holds up beautifully to the marinade, soaking up all the mouthwatering juices and transforming itself into irresistibly tender morsels. Most recipes for this dish call for plain white vinegar; instead, use the best sherry vinegar you can find.

4 TABLESPOONS VEGETABLE OIL

2 POUNDS SWORDFISH FILLET, CUT INTO 1-INCH CUBES

1 TABLESPOON COARSE SEA SALT,
PLUS MORE TO TASTE

1 TEASPOON FRESHLY GROUND BLACK PEPPER,
PLUS MORE TO TASTE

½ CUP ALL-PURPOSE FLOUR

1 MEDIUM RED BELL PEPPER, DICED

1 GREEN BELL PEPPER, DICED

1 MEDIUM RED ONION, DICED

8 BAY LEAVES (FRESH IF POSSIBLE)

1 TEASPOON CHOPPED FRESH GINGER

1 TEASPOON PAPRIKA

1 TABLESPOON MIXED PEPPERCORNS (OR WHITE)

2 TABLESPOONS MINCED PICKLED
(OR FRESH) HOT CHILI PEPPERS

1 CUP GREEN OLIVES, PITTED

½ CUP CAPERS, DRAINED

2 CUPS EXTRA-VIRGIN OLIVE OIL

1 CUP SHERRY VINEGAR

1. Heat the oil in a large skillet over medium flame. Season the fish cubes with the tablespoon of salt and the teaspoon of pepper, dredge them in the flour, and shake off the excess flour. Add to the skillet and sauté until golden brown on all sides, turning them over constantly, 1 minute on each side, until lightly browned.

2. Transfer the fish cubes to an ovenproof glass dish or glass storage container.

3. Add the peppers and onions to the skillet and sauté for 3 minutes, or until soft. Then add all the remaining ingredients, plus salt and pepper to taste, mix well, and then remove to a glass dish. (Add more oil and vinegar, in equal parts, if necessary to cover the solid ingredients.)

4. Allow the escabeche to cool, then cover and refrigerate it for at least 8 hours and up to 4 days. Serve at room temperature with toothpicks for easy pickup.

411: Simple Syrup

This cocktail sweetener can be made of varying thickness: thin is 3 parts water to 1 part sugar, medium is 2:1, and thick is 1:1. Simply bring the sugar and water to a boil, then remove from the heat immediately and set aside to cool. Store in a jar in the refrigerator for as long as you like.

Picadillo in a Lettuce Cup with Fresh Tomato Salsa

In assembling recipes for this Cuban extravaganza, I thought I'd like to have some kind of empanada, the little pastry turnover or patty found throughout the Caribbean and Latin America. They seemed labor-intensive, however, and a bit heavy. So we saved the stuffing and threw out the turkey. We borrowed a Vietnamese custom and placed the ground-beef mixture, called picadillo, in cups made of iceberg lettuce, and topped them with heirloom-tomato salsa to form exquisite bite-size packages. (Who wants to get weighed down by a lot of heavy fried dough anyway?)

2 tablespoons olive oil or vegetable oil
2 pounds lean ground beef
2 medium yellow onions, minced
4 garlic cloves, minced
1/2 cup chopped pimiento-stuffed green olives
1 cup raisins
2 tablespoons capers, drained
4 tablespoons white vinegar
1 cup Tomato Sauce (page 27)
1 teaspoon coarse sea salt
1/2 teaspoon freshly ground black pepper
2 large heads of iceberg lettuce
Fresh Tomato Salsa (recipe follows)

Fresh Tomato Salsa

1. Heat the oil in a large skillet over medium-high flame. Add the beef and sauté, stirring and breaking up with a wooden spoon for 5 minutes, until it's evenly browned with no lumps. Add the onions and cook for an additional 2 minutes, until they are soft. Add the garlic and cook for an additional 2 minutes, stirring occasionally.

2. Stir in the olives, raisins, capers, vinegar, and tomato sauce. Season with the salt and pepper. Lower the heat to medium-low, cover, and cook for 30 minutes.

3. Break off the outside leaves of the lettuce heads (see Note) and carefully pull out the inner curled leaves to form cups. Place them on a serving platter and fill each of them with about 2 table-spoons of the meat mixture. Top each mound of meat with a teaspoon of tomato salsa.

NOTE Leftover outside leaves of the lettuce can be reserved to make a salad. The leftover meat mixture can be topped with potatoes or sweet potatoes to make a shepherd's pie, or combined with tomato sauce to make a ragù for pasta.

The salsa is meant for two uses in our Cuban cocktail party: to top off the lettuce cups of picadillo, and as a dip for the fried tortillas (recipe follows). The recipe is best prepared in advance; make it the morning of the party, refrigerate for the day, and take it out 1 or 2 hours before serving.

5 large red heirloom tomatoes, chopped
5 large yellow heirloom tomatoes, chopped
1 medium red onion, chopped
1 4-ounce jar pimiento peppers,
cut into small cubes
1 fresh jalapeño pepper,
cored, seeded, and minced
Salt and freshly ground black pepper, to taste
1/3 cup olive oil
Splash of sherry vinegar

Mix all ingredients in a glass or other nonreactive bowl and serve at room temperature.

411: Heirloom Vegetables

Over the past thirty years, seed companies have been developing hybrids of vegetables that look good and hold up well under shipping conditions but do not necessarily maintain their essential or authentic flavors. In other words, they have been standardized and beautified, which has led to bland taste. In reaction to this trend, many growers who believed in natural or organic farming began to save the seeds from their crops to plant the next season rather than buy them from the seed companies. These heirloom seeds produce vegetables with more taste and character.

OTT: Freshly Fried Tortillas

Instead of offering store-bought fried or baked tortilla chips, buy fresh corn or flour tortillas, cut them into wedges, and deep-fry them in a light vegetable oil at 350°F. (They take about 5 to 8 minutes to turn a lovely golden color; so have a little patience and you will reap the rewards.) It's one of those simple ideas that immediately cranks your party up a notch and cements your reputation as a clever, resourceful host. The deep-fried fresh tortillas are plump, stylish, crispy, substantial —yet at the same time much lighter. The store-bought versions, even if they're of the so-called restaurant style variety, run a distant second.

When deep-frying, always drop items into the pot one by one. If you drop by the handful, they can stick together in an unattractive, difficult-to-handle bunch that is virtually impossible to separate. Furthermore, a bunch will drop the oil temperature significantly, and the cooler oil will be more readily absorbed by whatever you're cooking. You want the oil to cook but not penetrate the food, yielding a crisp result—not a heavy, soggy, oil-logged one.

411: Plantains

The plantain is a large, firm-fleshed banana popular in all the tropical cuisines of the Caribbean and Central America. Unlike other types of bananas, it is eaten cooked, not raw, and is usually served as a vegetable side dish. The banana is one of the few fruits that ripens better off the tree than on it, which of course makes it ideal for shipping to distant lands. The plantains suitable for frying or sautéing are yellow and black on the outside, like regular eating bananas. Firm, all-yellow ones are best for fried plantain chips. As they ripen, they turn a mottled yellow and black, and eventually all black, and soften and sweeten dramatically. Too mushy to create crisp chips, these very ripe ones are nevertheless delicious pan-fried and served as a side dish. The less-ripe green plantains are suitable only for stewing or boiling. Plantains are increasingly available in supermarkets. If you're unsure about them, ask at your local market.

OTT

For an authentic touch, add lard or coconut oil to your vegetable oil before frying. A little less healthy, of course, but a lot more flavorful.

The key here is to slice the plantains thinly and evenly, fry them in oil that is hot but not smoking, and drain them well. This way, they turn out crisp and crunchy, not soggy. The best way to slice them is with a mandoline. If you don't own one, do it carefully with a large, sharp kitchen knife. You can use the same pot and oil to deep-fry the bananas (see pages 49 and 105). Whatever you do, don't lose track of the oil temperature.

VEGETABLE OIL FOR DEEP-FRYING

3 YELLOW PLANTAINS,
SLICED CROSSWISE PAPER-THIN (1/8 INCH THICK)

SALT, TO TASTE

1. Fill a large heavy-bottomed pot to a depth of 3 to 4 inches with the oil. Place it on a burner over medium-high heat until the oil reaches a temperature of 350° F. (Use a candy thermometer to measure. If you don't have one, throw in a drop of water; if it sizzles immediately, the oil is hot enough. For more notes on deep-frying, see pages 49 and 105.) Lower the heat to medium. The temperature of the oil should not exceed 375°F.; don't allow it to begin smoking, or it will burn and produce unpleasant flavors.
2. As the oil reaches 350°F., use a slotted spoon to slide the plantain slices in one by one. Fry until golden brown (see Note), about 2 to 3 minutes. Remove cooked slices with the slotted spoon, season immediately with salt, and drain on paper towels.

NOTE You can fry the plantain chips in advance and, if they get a bit soggy waiting to be served, simply crisp them up by warming them in a 200° F. oven.

COLIN'S CUBAN SANDWICHES

This is a variation on the famous Cuban sandwich, which I Americanized and simplified. Using the best ingredients with a twist—Gruyère cheese, high-quality ham, and a parsley-mustard spread—makes it so much more than just a grilled ham-and-cheese sandwich. You'll find you can't make them fast enough: they're totally irresistible, warm and crunchy, and really too delicious for words. They also go exceedingly well with the cool drinks.

½ CUP DIJON MUSTARD
½ CUP FINELY CHOPPED FLAT-LEAF PARSLEY
24 SLICES WHITE SANDWICH BREAD
24 THIN SLICES GOOD-QUALITY GRUYÈRE
(OR OTHER SWISS) CHEESE
12 THICK SLICES GOOD-QUALITY BAKED HAM
2 STICKS (1 CUP) UNSALTED BUTTER, MELTED

1. Combine the mustard and parsley in a small bowl and mix well. Lay out 12 slices of the bread on a flat surface. Spread a layer of the mustard–parsley paste on each slice. Lay a slice of cheese and then a slice of ham on each one. Finish with another piece of cheese on each and then complete the sandwiches with the remaining slices of bread.

2. Melt the butter in a small saucepan over medium heat. Using a pastry brush, coat both sides of the sandwiches with butter. Heat a griddle over high heat. (You can also use a cast-iron skillet, but this doesn't yield the nice stripes.) Grill the sandwiches until the bread turns golden brown and the cheese is well melted, 3 to 4 minutes on each side. Cut in quarters and serve hot.

Arroz con Camarones

Another big hit is this shrimp-and-rice recipe adapted from a classic, *arroz con pollo* (chicken and rice). I find this dish has the most impact visually when it's served in small portions in espresso cups.

You can create several interesting variations on this recipe: Try adding mussels, clams, and cut-up fish fillets to make a paella. Substitute cubes of lean chicken breast for the shrimp. Or remove the bacon and do a vegetarian version. There is also an alternate method of preparation: The instructions below call for baking the ingredients, paella-style, but you might choose to cook the rice and other ingredients well in advance without the shrimp. Then, just before serving, fry the shrimp separately in 2 tablespoons of oil over medium-high heat for 1 to 2 minutes, and combine them with the rice mixture.

¼ POUND DICED APPLEWOOD-SMOKED BACON

1 MEDIUM YELLOW ONION, DICED

1 RED BELL PEPPER, DICED

1 YELLOW BELL PEPPER, DICED

1 ORANGE BELL PEPPER, DICED (IF AVAILABLE;
IF NOT, ADD ANOTHER RED OR YELLOW, BUT NOT GREEN)

3 GARLIC CLOVES, MINCED (ABOUT 2 TABLESPOONS)

2 CUPS CONVERTED SHORT-GRAIN RICE

1 TABLESPOON COARSE SALT

1 TEASPOON FRESHLY GROUND BLACK PEPPER

½ CUP WHITE WINE

½ CUP TOMATO PURÉE

2 CUPS CHICKEN STOCK (PAGE 120)
OR VEGETABLE STOCK

½ TEASPOON DRIED OREGANO

½ TEASPOON GROUND CUMIN

¼ TEASPOON CRUSHED HOT RED PEPPER FLAKES

2 BAY LEAVES

½ TEASPOON SAFFRON THREADS

2 POUNDS MEDIUM SHRIMP (18 TO 20 PER POUND),
SHELLED AND DEVEINED

CHOPPED FLAT-LEAF PARSLEY, FOR GARNISH

1. Preheat the oven to 400°F.
2. Heat a large sauté pan, skillet, paella pan, or other wide shallow pan over medium flame. Add the bacon, onion, and peppers, and sauté for about 5 minutes, or until soft. Add the garlic and rice. Stir until the rice is well coated. Add the remaining ingredients except for the shrimp and parsley. Bring to a boil, then cover the pan and place in the oven to bake for 20 minutes.
3. While the rice bakes, bring a medium pot of water to a boil.

Add the shrimp and cook until just done, about 3 minutes. Drain and run under cold water to halt cooking.
4. Remove the rice from the oven, stir in the shrimp, garnish with parsley, and serve.

Fried Bananas with Caramel Sauce

Here is the Cuban cocktail-party version of dessert. Since the menu is built around bite-size portions of food presented on trays, this is a natural choice for the finale. You'll love the scrumptious contrast between the sweet, melted bananas and their crispy fried batter—not to mention the decadent caramel sauce.

2 cups all-purpose flour

3 large eggs, separated

¾ cup lager beer

Pinch of salt

¼ cup vegetable oil

2 tablespoons sugar

Vegetable oil for deep-frying

6 large bananas, peeled and cut into 1-inch sections

Confectioners' sugar

Caramel Sauce (recipe follows)

1. In a large mixing bowl, combine the flour, egg yolks, beer, salt, and oil. Whisk together until a smooth batter forms with no lumps. Allow to rest for 1 hour at room temperature.

2. In another bowl, whip the egg white with a whisk and gradually add the sugar until the mixture forms soft peaks. Fold into the batter.

3. In a large cast-iron skillet or Dutch oven, heat 3 to 4 inches of vegetable oil until it reaches a temperature of 350°F. (use a candy thermometer). Using a wooden skewer or large toothpick, dip the banana pieces in the batter, add one by one to the hot oil, and fry until golden brown, 1 to 2 minutes. Throughout the frying, be sure that the oil is at least 350°F. but not exceeding 375°F. Drain the browned bananas on paper towels. Sprinkle them with confectioners' sugar and serve with the caramel sauce poured on top or on the side for dipping.

Caramel Sauce

1 cup sugar

¼ cup water

Place 1 cup of sugar in a medium saucepan over medium heat. Make sure the pot is large enough to avoid splashing; the sauce will bubble when the water is added. Melt the sugar without stirring until it turns a deep caramel color. (The sugar will turn color quickly; do not burn it.) Slowly add ¼ cup of water, stirring carefully so as not to splash.

On Fire
for 8

Several years ago I received a call from my dear friend Jim Block, who is also a very talented lighting designer with a great sense of style; he has lit many of the more dramatic parties I've organized around the world. Jim asked me to come look at a house he was about to purchase in the Hollywood Hills. He wanted my opinion; I took one look at the place and simply replied, "Jim, if you don't buy it, I will." In fact, I was so enamored of the house that I ended up helping him remodel it, and I took on the role of interior designer. So when it came time to arrange a few dinner parties in L.A., Jim's house was at the top of my list.

In my travels around the world, whenever I'm in shopping mode, I've always kept Jim's house in mind. I've bought choice items anytime I see them—just the right pieces to fit the aesthetic—and helped him assemble his collection of household objects and art.

For this particular occasion, it's a casual gathering of friends and neighbors: the actress Leila Kenzel and her husband the writer Neil Monaco; my South African friends Brendan Kerzner and his fiancée, Christine; and two actor friends, Rick Otto and Vanessa Angel.

Outdoor summer barbecues are a time-honored tradition— practically a sacred ritual—in America. This meal is modest, streamlined, and gratifying. Marinating a good piece of meat well in advance and then simply grilling it is a sure-fire recipe for success. This is an early-summer get-together, hence the choice of lamb. The meal is served family-style. I cleared one end of the table, leaving it open to arrange the platters like a buffet and to showcase a handsome wooden bowl full of red and green apples.

As a host, the best question you can ask yourself is, "How do I make my guests feel more welcome?" For an evening party, one way to accomplish this is to create a special lighting accent in the entryway. You can place candles in the hallway, lanterns on the stairs leading to your door or on the porch; even a couple of small votive candles on a side table or in an alcove say "Good evening and welcome to my party" better than almost anything else. Colored candles, particularly red, always signal a warm, sexy hello. For this party, we also placed red glass mosaic lanterns coming down the stairs at the entryway to the house—an extra welcoming touch.

411: A Well-Stocked Bar

I'm a big believer in having a well-stocked bar. It gives you flexibility and spontaneity; there's a continual cocktail party waiting to happen at a moment's notice. A well-stocked bar should also feature variety—that is, every category of alcohol, mixer, and glass you can imagine. If you decide right now to start collecting bit by bit, steadily acquiring an item or two here and there, you'll be surprised how soon you'll have a complete kit. And it will become a key element in your entertainment strategy.

The Menu: Supper for Eight

Appetizer
Cucumber, Tomato, and Feta Salad

Main Course
Grilled Butterflied Leg of Lamb
Grilled Vegetables with
Shallot-Lemon-Soy Vinaigrette

Dessert
S'mores

To Drink
Cocktail de Nuit: Strepe Chepe
Wine: Châteauneuf-du-Pape
THE FULL-BODIED, SPICY, FRUITY, LONG-LASTING RED FROM THE FAMOUS SOUTHERN-RHÔNE APPELLATION. IT COMBINES THE BEST OF RUSTIC COUNTRY VILLAGE WINES AND THEIR UPSCALE SOPHISTICATED COUNTERPARTS, AND FINDS A SUPERB MATCH WITH HEARTY GRILLED MEATS SUCH AS THIS LAMB.

TIMING Prepare the salad in advance and allow it to chill in the fridge or freezer before serving. The lamb is a simple, quick preparation, but it needs to be marinated in advance; this can be done either the night before or the morning of. The great thing about this dinner is that everything past the first-course salad is done on the grill. Once you've grilled the vegetables and the lamb, you can cover the grill to conserve the coals so they'll burn low and gently melt the dessert. Have the chocolate-marshmallow sandwiches (s'mores) prepared in advance so all you have to do at the end of the main course is cover the grill rack with foil and put them on to melt the chocolate and marshmallows.

Strepe Chepe

This is a fabulous, refreshing, and potent concoction, which is ideal for launching a summer party. I discovered it courtesy of my friends Sloan and Roger Barnett. One of my favorite things about it is its subtle green color. The tricky thing about frozen drinks like this one is you don't taste the alcohol—they give such a fresh, innocent impression but they can sneak up on you. So be careful, and enjoy!

8 OUNCES HIGH-QUALITY VODKA

2 TABLESPOONS FRESH LIME JUICE

3 TABLESPOONS SUPERFINE SUGAR,
PLUS MORE TO TASTE

1/2 CUP FRESH MINT LEAVES, TIGHTLY PACKED

Combine all the ingredients in a blender full of ice cubes. Blend until the contents achieve a uniform frozen consistency. Add more sugar periodically as needed or until the mixture is just sweet to the taste. Serve in champagne flutes.

Cucumber, Tomato, and Feta Salad

This light salad is served well chilled, which makes it a refreshing first course for a summer barbecue. The feta cheese and black olives provide a Mediterranean accent that continues with the lamb.

6 MEDIUM TOMATOES (ORGANIC IF POSSIBLE),
PEELED (SEE NOTE), SEEDED, AND CUT INTO 1/2-INCH CUBES

2 LARGE ENGLISH (SEEDLESS) CUCUMBERS,
PEELED AND CUT INTO 1/2-INCH CUBES

1/4 POUND PITTED BLACK OLIVES

1 1/2 POUNDS FETA CHEESE, CUT INTO 1 1/4-INCH CUBES

2 TABLESPOONS CHOPPED FRESH BASIL

4 TABLESPOONS RICE VINEGAR

1 TABLESPOON SUGAR

4 TABLESPOONS EXTRA-VIRGIN OLIVE OIL

COARSE SEA SALT AND FRESHLY
GROUND BLACK PEPPER, TO TASTE

In a large bowl, combine the tomatoes, cucumbers, olives, feta, and basil, and mix well. To make the dressing, mix the vinegar and sugar together in a small bowl, then gradually whisk in the olive oil. Add the dressing to the salad, season with salt and pepper, and toss well. Place the salad in the refrigerator for 1 hour or the freezer for 15 minutes before serving.

NOTE To peel tomatoes, use a paring knife to score them with an "X" mark on top. (The center of the "X" should be the spot where the stem was plucked.) Drop the tomatoes in a pot of boiling water for 30 seconds, plunge them immediately into ice water to stop any cooking action, then peel off the skins by hand.

GRILLED BUTTERFLIED LEG OF LAMB

A whole leg of lamb is generally either roasted on the bone or deboned, then stuffed and rolled for roasting. Here is the other delicious alternative: leaving it butterflied (boned and opened up flat) so it can be marinated and grilled quickly. The classic Greek marinade for leg of lamb would contain olive oil, garlic, oregano, and lemon; in this recipe, inspired by my friend Jonathan Beere, we add parsley and rosemary along with some Dijon mustard to take it on a slightly French trajectory. Feel free to try either variation or to create your own.

I CUP FRESH FLAT-LEAF PARSLEY LEAVES
I CUP FRESH ROSEMARY LEAVES, STEMMED
2 TABLESPOONS FRESHLY GROUND BLACK PEPPER
I 2 GARLIC CLOVES, PEELED
4 TEASPOONS DIJON MUSTARD
3 TABLESPOONS EXTRA-VIRGIN OLIVE OIL
I (6-POUND) DEBONED, BUTTERFLIED LEG OF LAMB
2 TABLESPOONS COARSE SALT,
PLUS MORE FOR GARNISH
4 LEMONS, QUARTERED, FOR GARNISH

1. **Prepare the marinade:** Place the parsley, rosemary, pepper, garlic, mustard, and olive oil in a food processor. Pulse until the mixture is the consistency of a smooth paste, about 1 minute. Rub the mixture all over the lamb, place the meat on a tray, cover with plastic wrap, and refrigerate for up to 12 hours.
2. Build a charcoal fire in a kettle-style grill or light a covered gas grill. Season the lamb all over with the salt. When the coals are medium-hot, place the lamb in the center of the rack, cover the grill, and cook for 20 minutes. Turn the lamb and cook for an additional 15 minutes. (To test for doneness, insert a meat thermometer into the center of the cut; 125° to 130°F. is medium rare. Otherwise, use the "fingertip test": see page 198.) When the meat is done, transfer it to a serving platter, loosely cover it with aluminum foil, and allow it to rest for 10 minutes before carving (see 411). Garnish the platter with the lemon quarters and serve with coarse sea salt on the side.

411: Resting

Most cuts of meat—even poultry—that are roasted or grilled benefit from a resting period after they've been taken off the heat. They should be placed on a platter or left in their pan and lightly covered with aluminum foil. This allows the internal juices, which tend to leach out during cooking, to seep back inside and permeate the whole cut while the exterior remains deliciously browned, caramelized, even crispy. The most succulent juices are quite runny when hot; as the meat gradually cools, they begin to coagulate inside the meat to keep it moist and juicy.

The resting period also allows a cut to become more evenly done, as the cooking process continues, then gradually tails off. The internal temperature of a large cut of meat, when allowed to rest, can easily increase 5 to 10 degrees during resting. So be sure to take the meat off the heat slightly cooler than your target temperature. Large roasts should be allowed to rest for 20 to 30 minutes before serving; steaks and chops (1 to 3 inches thick) for 5 to 10 minutes.

911

To cook the leg of lamb in the oven, place it in a broiler pan on the middle rack and broil for 15 minutes on each side. Remove from the oven and allow to stand for 10 minutes before carving.

GRILLED VEGETABLES WITH SHALLOT-LEMON-SOY VINAIGRETTE

There's nothing quite as straightforward and delicious as grilled fresh vegetables. I think too many people forget this option when they're barbecuing outdoors in the summer; they make the mistake of trying to prepare something more elaborate in the kitchen, and they're caught juggling too many balls in the air at once.

6 JAPANESE EGGPLANTS, HALVED LENGTHWISE
6 MEDIUM ZUCCHINI, HALVED LENGTHWISE
12 SCALLIONS (2 BUNCHES)
EXTRA-VIRGIN OLIVE OIL FOR BRUSHING (ABOUT 1 CUP)
1 TABLESPOON COARSE SEA SALT
1/2 TABLESPOON FRESHLY GROUND BLACK PEPPER
SHALLOT-LEMON-SOY VINAIGRETTE (RECIPE FOLLOWS)

1. Brush the vegetables with the olive oil and season with the salt and pepper. Place the vegetables on a preheated grill and cook, uncovered, for about 10 minutes, until slightly soft but still crunchy and marked by the grill.

2. Cut each of the vegetables into three sections, place them in a bowl or on a serving platter, drizzle with some shallot-lemon-soy vinaigrette, and serve.

SHALLOT-LEMON-SOY VINAIGRETTE

2 TABLESPOONS FRESH LEMON JUICE
(FROM 1 MEDIUM LEMON)
2 TABLESPOONS SOY SAUCE
1 TEASPOON MINCED FRESH GINGER
1 TABLESPOON MINCED SHALLOTS
1/2 CUP OLIVE OIL
1 TEASPOON SALT
1/2 TEASPOON FRESHLY GROUND BLACK PEPPER

Combine the lemon juice, soy sauce, ginger, and shallots in a small mixing bowl. Gradually whisk in the oil. Season with the salt and pepper.

S'MORES

For the carb-conscious dieters among us, this meal is absolutely no threat up to this point. Then comes dessert, which is an exercise in the sweet, sinful nostalgia of childhood for anyone who grew up in America during the past thirty years or so. Of course, the s'mores, so called for obvious reasons, are entirely optional; but like any really good sweet, I find them extremely difficult to resist. So splurge a bit, enjoy life for an evening, and spend a few extra minutes at the gym tomorrow.

16 GRAHAM CRACKERS
4 (7-OUNCE) BARS OF GOOD-QUALITY
MILK CHOCOLATE, HALVED
16 MARSHMALLOWS, HALVED

1. Prepare the sandwiches: Each consists of 2 graham crackers with half a chocolate bar and 4 marshmallow halves in between.
2. Cover the grill rack with a piece of aluminum foil large enough to hold all the sandwiches. (The fire should be fairly low by this point, as chocolate needs to be melted quite slowly; the aluminum foil will also protect the chocolate from scorching, which ruins its flavor.) Place the sandwiches on the foil, cover the grill, and cook until the chocolate and marshmallows are melted through, 4 to 5 minutes. Serve hot with vanilla ice cream.

OTT
Serve the s'mores with vanilla ice cream on the side.

911
To melt the s'mores in the oven, place them on the bottom rack at 350°F. for 10 minutes.

DINING IN THE HEARTH
FOR 4

It's Tuesday, four o'clock, the end of a chilly, overcast late-winter afternoon. You've been slaving at your desk for hours, and you're in the mood for some company this evening. You get on the phone with Prudence, whom you haven't seen in what feels like ages. "What are you doing for dinner tonight?" you ask. She suggests a restaurant. You say, "Forget it, I dined out at Town last night. Come on over. We'll have dinner in the kitchen. Bring a fabulous bottle of red wine and I'll cook something fabulous."

I try to do as much spontaneous, last-minute entertaining as possible. There's nothing as enjoyable as an impromptu home-cooked meal with friends. But to do it, it's absolutely essential to have several reliable, easy, tasty dishes up your sleeve. This menu showcases a few of my favorites. The evening is chic and simple, unpretentious and unexpected. It's not about fancy food or expensive accessories. Take, for example, the candles, which I purchased a year ago for one of my television shows: They're attractive, and they burn forever.

The recipes are updated, quick-and-easy versions of several classics—with my edge. When you think of comfort food, it's generally for a winter or cold-weather meal. In this case, I injected a traditional note of spring with the asparagus, which is now available year round in most markets.

Like anybody who loves to cook, I spend a lot of time in my kitchen. A few years ago, I decided to transform the space with an eye toward entertaining. The walls were creamy white; the cabinets were dark wood—typical for a pre-war New York City apartment. I painted the walls with several layers of oxblood red, giving them a lacquered finish that's easy to keep clean. I rolled out some Turkish rugs and suspended an overscaled Turkish eye for good luck over the kitchen sink. (It was a gift from my friend Hakan Ezer from Istanbul.) I put four barstools around the stainless-steel work table in the middle of the room and acquired small tablecloths in myriad colors. I also installed a couple of speakers hooked up to my main music system. Now I dine there at least once a day. All I have to do is put on my favorite new CD, and adjust the dimmer switch, and I've magically transformed what was once a strictly utilitarian room into an intimate dining space.

I always try to think graphically when I'm arranging a tabletop. In this case, I created a kind of organic fire-and-earth checkerboard. First, I placed a couple of sapling trees in terra-cotta pots and transplanted some live moss balls from plastic containers into rocks glasses. (You can find these types of items at any nursery or flower shop.) I filled the empty spaces with black square-pillar candles, creating a look that is contemporary and cool, almost like a self-contained miniature Japanese garden.

KEEP IT SIMPLE

One of the classic mistakes many people make is they try to get too complicated. They think that by adding ingredients, by making more complex recipes, they're making a better party. Wrong. The more complicated a recipe, the greater the margin for error. I'm a firm believer that whenever you cook, you should take the world's finest ingredients and do as little to them as possible. Keep the recipes simple and focus on the occasion. See the big picture; plan the details.

411: Candles

I always try to keep a lot of candles on hand. They're warm and welcoming, and they send an immediate message to your guests: You're at the party now, you're out of the harsh daylight and the fluorescent buzz of the office. It's time to sit back, relax, and have some fun. I like to use fragrant candles for the bathroom. (Don't use them in the dining room; they may clash with food and wine aromas, and you don't want your Château Margaux smelling like gardenias!) I love the thick, square box candles: They're inexpensive, available at many housewares stores, and long-lasting. They also provide beautiful color accents and sculptural elements for any table arrangement. I particularly like dimming the lights and placing candles in the entry space to any apartment or house. It's the first thing the guests see when they arrive, and it helps them downshift into party gear immediately.

The Menu: Supper for Four

Appetizer
Mixed Asparagus with Vinaigrette

Main Course
Homemade Meatloaf with Mushroom Gravy
Sautéed Green Beans (optional)
Macaroni and Cheese

Dessert
Triple Chocolate Delight

To Drink
Wine and Coffee
No need to serve elaborate cocktails with this meal. We had a nice bottle of South African cabernet sauvignon—before the meal and with the main course, though not with the asparagus; they clash. For the chocolate dessert, a demitasse of good coffee is an excellent option.

TIMING This is a super-relaxed meal where the guests can sit in the kitchen and enjoy a glass of wine while I'm completing my last-minute preparations. The total preparation time is less than two hours. Make the cake in advance (or buy it already made). Prepare the meatloaf earlier and put it in the oven well before the guests arrive. Then proceed with the macaroni and cheese, the asparagus, and the beans (optional).

Nesting

The harder we work, the more fragmented and capitalistic our society becomes, the more we want to go back to nesting. Nesting is about enjoying our home as a place of refuge from all the noise and bustle outside; it's about preparing comfort food for an intimate gathering in the kitchen or den. Entertaining at home can be so much more meaningful than large cocktail parties and sit-down dinners for eight or more.

NOTE Place the asparagus in a bowl of cold water to preserve their freshness while peeling them.

Mixed Asparagus with Vinaigrette

I use a couple of simple touches to jazz up this "standard." First, I select two types of asparagus for visual appeal. Second, I add a dash of truffle oil to the vinaigrette, which already possesses an inherent richness from the walnut oil; with essence of truffle it soars to new heights.

FOR THE ASPARAGUS

2 tablespoons coarse salt

1 teaspoon sugar

2 bunches (approximately 16 spears or 1 pound) of medium-large white asparagus, woody stems trimmed and peeled (see 411), tied with white kitchen twine

2 bunches (approximately 16 spears or 1 pound) of medium-large green asparagus, woody stems trimmed and peeled (see 411), tied with white kitchen twine

FOR THE VINAIGRETTE

2 tablespoons Dijon mustard

1/2 teaspoon salt

1/4 teaspoon freshly ground black pepper

1/3 cup sherry vinegar

1/3 cup plus 2 tablespoons walnut oil

2/3 cup vegetable oil
(such as canola or grapeseed oil)

1. Add the salt and sugar to a large pot of water and bring to a boil. Add the white asparagus and cook over medium heat for 15 minutes, until tender. Remove with tongs to a colander, refresh with cold running water, drain well, and set aside.

2. Add the green asparagus to the same pot of boiling water and cook for 5 to 6 minutes, or until tender. Remove, drain in a colander, refresh with cold running water, drain well, and set aside. (Be sure to cook the white asparagus first; otherwise, it may turn greenish in the other's cooking water.)

3. Meanwhile, make the vinaigrette: In a blender, combine the mustard, salt, pepper, and vinegar. With the motor running on low, gradually add the oils until the mixture emulsifies; the oils should be added very slowly in order to render the dressing thick and creamy. Adjust the seasonings to taste.

4. Divide the asparagus into 4 equal portions (approximately 8 stalks each), arrange on plates, and dress generously with the vinaigrette.

HOMEMADE MEATLOAF WITH MUSHROOM GRAVY

The key here is baking the meatloaf in a terrine or loaf pan—its dimensions should be $10 \times 3 \times 3$ inches. This serves the dual purpose of keeping it moist (the juices are held in) and making it eminently presentable.

2 SLICES SOFT WHITE SANDWICH BREAD

1 CUP WHOLE MILK

2 TABLESPOONS UNSALTED BUTTER

1/2 CUP FINELY CHOPPED ONION
(FROM 1 MEDIUM ONION)

1/4 CUP FINELY CHOPPED CARROT
(FROM 1 SMALL CARROT)

1/4 CUP FINELY CHOPPED CELERY
(FROM 1 STALK OF CELERY)

2 GARLIC CLOVES, MINCED

1 TABLESPOON COARSE SEA SALT

1 TEASPOON FRESHLY GROUND BLACK PEPPER

1/2 TEASPOON DRIED RED PEPPER FLAKES

2 LARGE EGGS

1/4 CUP KETCHUP

1/4 CUP DIJON MUSTARD

2 POUNDS GROUND BEEF

2 TABLESPOONS CHOPPED FRESH PARSLEY

1 TABLESPOON CHOPPED FRESH BASIL

1 TEASPOON CHOPPED FRESH THYME

1/2 TEASPOON CHOPPED FRESH ROSEMARY

1. Preheat the oven to 350°F.

2. Cut the crust off the slices of bread. In a small bowl, soak the bread in the milk for 15 minutes, then drain and squeeze to remove excess liquid.

3. Melt the butter in a saucepan over medium-low heat. Add the onion, carrot, celery, and garlic. Cook 10 minutes, or until the vegetables are soft. Remove from the heat and allow to cool.

4. Combine the sautéed vegetables with all the other ingredients in a large mixing bowl. Mix by hand until all the ingredients are well incorporated.

5. Fill the terrine pan with the meat mixture. Place the terrine in a slightly larger baking pan to catch any dripping grease. Bake in the middle part of the preheated oven for 1 hour and 10 minutes. Use a toothpick test to determine doneness: When the juice runs clear and the toothpick comes out clean, the meatloaf is ready. Serve with the mushroom gravy (recipe follows).

411: Asparagus

• Asparagus is a member of the lily family, whose natural growing season is late winter through early summer.

• Most asparagus is green, although there is a purple variety and also the white, which is picked shortly after it pokes its tips aboveground and before it develops chlorophyll (responsible for a plant's green color).

• Asparagus stems (or spears) come in different sizes, from pencil-thin to jumbo-thick. The older a plant is, the thicker stems it produces. Thicker stems from older plants can be tough on the outside and should be peeled with a vegetable peeler.

• To prepare for cooking, trim the blunt ends to an even length and peel the tough outer layer as necessary with a vegetable peeler.

• Asparagus can be steamed as an alternative to boiling.

• It takes almost four times longer to cook white asparagus than it does green, because the white has more stringy, tough connective tissue.

• While peeling, place asparagus in water to preserve freshness.

OTT

Add a tablespoon of truffle oil to the vinaigrette.

SAUTÉED GREEN BEANS

Haricots verts, of course, is French for "green beans." The French variety is a *true* string bean—smaller, more delicate, greener, and definitely better than the thick ones.

I TABLESPOON PLUS ¼ TEASPOON SALT
I POUND HARICOTS VERTS
2 TABLESPOONS UNSALTED BUTTER
I SHALLOT, MINCED
I GARLIC CLOVE, MINCED
¼ TEASPOON FRESHLY GROUND BLACK PEPPER

1. Place 1 tablespoon of the salt in a large pot of water and bring to a boil (see Note). Add the beans and cook over medium heat until tender but still slightly crunchy (al dente), about 4 minutes. Drain in a colander and refresh under cold water to halt cooking.
2. While the beans are cooking, melt the butter in a large sauté pan over medium-low heat, add the shallot and garlic, and cook for 1 to 2 minutes, or until soft. Add the drained beans, toss, season with the ¼ teaspoon each of the salt and pepper, and serve.

NOTE Instead of boiling, you can steam the beans for 3 to 4 minutes in a medium-size pot equipped with a vegetable steamer. Remove the lid from the pot after 2 minutes to preserve the beans' green color. Once they are steamed, proceed with step 2.

MUSHROOM GRAVY

2 TABLESPOONS UNSALTED BUTTER
½ MEDIUM YELLOW ONION, DICED (ABOUT ½ CUP)
½ POUND WHITE BUTTON MUSHROOMS,
RINSED, PATTED DRY, AND THINLY SLICED
2 TABLESPOONS ALL-PURPOSE FLOUR
I TEASPOON COARSE SALT
½ TEASPOON FRESHLY GROUND BLACK PEPPER
2 CUPS VEAL STOCK (PAGE I 86)
OR CHICKEN STOCK (PAGE I 20)

1. Melt the butter in a medium saucepan over medium heat. Add the onion and sauté for 2 minutes, or until soft. Add the mushrooms and sauté until golden brown, about 5 minutes. Add the flour and cook 1 to 2 minutes, stirring constantly.
2. Add the stock and allow to come to a boil. Add the salt and pepper, and continue to boil until thickened, 5 to 10 minutes. Adjust the seasoning and serve.

OTT

During truffle season, shave some white truffles onto the macaroni and cheese and serve as a separate course between the asparagus and the meatloaf. Or add some crispy fried pancetta or bacon for another note.

MACARONI AND CHEESE

This is the ultimate comfort food, truly nurturing and delicious. To give it an edge of extra richness, I suggest a top-quality imported Gruyère cheese. You could buy a standard supermarket-quality Cheddar or Monterey Jack but, trust me, there is a difference; with Gruyère, the result is superior in both flavor and consistency.

I POUND ZITI
(OR OTHER SMALL TUBE-SHAPED PASTA)

I TEASPOON COARSE SALT,
PLUS MORE FOR THE PASTA WATER

I CUP WHOLE MILK

2 CUPS HEAVY CREAM

2 GARLIC CLOVES, MINCED

2 CUPS GRATED GRUYÈRE CHEESE
(FROM ABOUT ½ POUND)

½ CUP GRATED PARMIGIANO-REGGIANO CHEESE
(FROM ABOUT 2 OUNCES)

½ TEASPOON FRESHLY GROUND BLACK PEPPER,
PLUS MORE TO TASTE

BUTTER FOR GREASING PAN

1. Preheat the oven to 375°F.
2. Cook the pasta in a large pot of salted boiling water until halfway done, about 6 minutes; do not overcook. Drain well and transfer to a large mixing bowl.
3. Meanwhile, place the milk, cream, and garlic in the same pot over medium heat and bring to a boil. Add the cooked pasta in the mixing bowl. Add 1 cup of the grated Gruyère plus the ½ cup of grated Parmigiano-Reggiano to the bowl and mix well. Season with salt and pepper.
4. Butter an ovenproof glass dish approximately 8 × 12 × 13 inches, transfer the pasta mixture to the dish, and sprinkle the remaining Gruyère evenly on top. Bake for 30 minutes (see Note), or until crispy and golden on top.

NOTE The macaroni and cheese can be baked for just 10 minutes and then set aside and finished later for 20 minutes.

411: Hazelnuts

Once their hard outer shell has been removed, hazelnuts still have a seed coating or husk that has a bitter taste. The best way to remove it is to toast the nuts at 350°F. for about 10 minutes; then they can be rubbed together in a towel or napkin, and the husks will flake off.

911

Use store-bought brownies or some other kind of chocolate cake if you're in a rush.

OTT

Place a chocolate truffle on top of the cake and suddenly your trio becomes a quartet!

911

Instead of the cocoa powder and grated chocolate, buy a large bar of high-quality semisweet chocolate. Break into medium-sized pieces, place in a double boiler over medium-high heat, and stir in skim milk as it melts until you have the desired consistency. Once melted, turn down the heat to low and keep warm until ready to serve. (Note: The water in the bottom pan of a double boiler should not be touching the top pan. Otherwise, the top pan gets too hot and the contents don't melt evenly.)

TRIPLE CHOCOLATE DELIGHT

How's this for a decadent finale? My favorite ice cream for this sinful trio is Godiva's Chocolate Hazelnut Truffle. If anything's going to send you over the top, it will. Any good chocolate ice cream will do, but this one is the best in my opinion. Despite the decadence, this cake is easy to prepare; all the mixing is done in a food processor with the steel blade attached. For a lighter touch, substitute chocolate sorbet for the ice cream.

FOR THE CAKE

BUTTER FOR GREASING THE PAN
1/2 CUP SEMISWEET CHOCOLATE MORSELS
1/2 CUP BLANCHED WHOLE ALMONDS
1 STICK (1/4 POUND) PLUS 2 TABLESPOONS BUTTER
1/2 CUP GRANULATED SUGAR
2 LARGE EGGS
SCANT 1/2 CUP ALL-PURPOSE FLOUR
1 TABLESPOON DUTCH-PROCESS COCOA
DASH OF SALT
1/2 CUP SHELLED HAZELNUTS,
TOASTED AND COARSELY CHOPPED
2 TABLESPOONS CONFECTIONERS' SUGAR,
TO SPRINKLE AS GARNISH
1 PINT CHOCOLATE ICE CREAM (SEE HEADNOTE)
1 BATCH CHOCOLATE SAUCE (RECIPE FOLLOWS)
PARCHMENT PAPER FOR LINING THE PAN

1. Preheat the oven to 400°F.
2. Grease an 8 × 8-inch baking pan or ovenproof dish with butter. Line with parchment paper, then coat the paper with butter.
3. Combine the chocolate morsels and the almonds in the bowl of a food processor fitted with the metal blade. Pulse about 10 times, or until the almonds and chocolate are ground into fine morsels. Set aside.
4. Combine the stick of butter and the granulated sugar in the food processor and process until light and fluffy. Add the eggs, one at a time, and continue processing. Add the reserved chocolate mixture and continue processing. Add the flour until all the ingredients are well combined.
5. Place 1/4 cup water in a saucepan over medium heat. Bring the water almost to a simmer. Stir in the cocoa and salt until dissolved. Remove from the heat and allow to cool slightly, then add to the bowl of the food processor, and process until well blended. Fold in the hazelnuts.

6. Pour the batter into the prepared pan and bake for 55 to 60 minutes, until a toothpick inserted in the center comes out clean. Cool in the pan or on a rack for 1 hour.
7. Cut the cake into individual portions. Place each portion in the center of a plate. To serve, sprinkle the cake with the confectioners' sugar, place a scoop of chocolate ice cream on each cake, and pour chocolate sauce on top.

CHOCOLATE SAUCE

2/3 CUP SUGAR
1 CUP UNSWEETENED COCOA POWDER
4 OUNCES SEMISWEET CHOCOLATE, GRATED
2 TABLESPOONS RUM

1. Place 1 cup water, the sugar, and the cocoa powder in a small saucepan over medium heat. Stir until the sugar is dissolved.
2. Reduce the heat to low, then add the grated chocolate and the rum. Stir the sauce until it is very smooth. If you make it in advance, keep it warm in a double boiler over medium-low heat until ready to serve.

In the Souk
for 6

Every great party is a journey, and tonight we explore the irresistible allure of the Moroccan souk . . .

If you haven't had the exquisite pleasure of visiting Morocco, you may be wondering what a souk is: a covered marketplace in the heart of the medina (the old city center); in Marrakech, the souk goes by the exotic name Djemaa El Fna. I've always loved traveling in Morocco, and this is one of my favorite spots in the country. Here's a dinner that transports you to that magical place in an instant.

"Marrakech!" The word rolls magically off your tongue, and the place looks exactly as it sounds. Nowhere else in the world is the sky bluer or the earth redder. You smell it in the air; you see it all around you. There's an incredible buzz, a palpable energy, in the city and in the medina, where hundreds of vendors sell everything from *djellabahs* and kaftans to olives, preserved lemons, and a huge array of exotic spices. I find it very exotic—its architecture, interior design, color palette, furniture, frenetic energy, and most definitely its food.

When it came to selecting a location for this intimate feast, my very dear friends Sloan and Roger Barnett offered their dining room, which is painted with trompe-l'oeil murals to look as if you're in the souk, inspired by their love of Morocco; I've enjoyed many a dinner in this great room. I encouraged our guests to dress *à la marocain,* which added an extra element of fun to the proceedings.

Part of the excitement of a theme dinner such as this is that you can get as carried away as you like and overproduce with no risk of looking silly. I kept this occasion relatively simple, though I couldn't resist one over-the-top idea for the buffet table: a large conical tower of dried fruit. (Hint: Its frame is a polystyrene cone with toothpicks inserted at the back of the fruits to hold them in place.)

Although Moroccan food can be quite labor intensive, I've extracted a couple of recipes that are easy to prepare and allow you to perform most of the steps in advance. In addition, several of the items are readily found in grocery stores.

Among my most-beloved cuisines—North African, Middle Eastern, Indian, and East Asian—one of the aspects I love best is the communal dining. Serving dishes fill the middle of the table and are passed around family style, which enhances the camaraderie of the occasion.

The Menu: Supper for Six

Appetizer Buffet
Marinated Olives and cherry Tomatoes
Hummus

Main Course
Artichokes Stuffed with Peas
Tagine of Chicken
Moroccan Tomato and Eggplant Salad
Couscous with Dried Fruits and Walnuts

Dessert
Strawberries and Orange Slices in
Orange-Blossom Water with Mint

To Drink
Cocktail de Nuit: Orange-and-Cardamom Martini
Wine: Provençal Red
Domaine Tempier's Bandol, arguably the finest wine
from Provence, offers a pleasantly dusty quality,
earthiness, good body, and hints of jammy blackberry
and bright cherry.
Dessert: Sweet Mint Tea

TIMING Both of the appetizer recipes I'm suggesting here can and should be made in advance. The olives and tomatoes need at least an hour to marinate. The hummus can be made in a large batch and refrigerated; it's ready to use as needed. So make the appetizers the morning of the party or the night before. The stuffed artichokes can be prepped in advance and warmed up just before serving, or made just before the guests are scheduled to arrive. The tomato and eggplant salad—which I serve here as a side dish but which can be presented as an appetizer as well—takes about an hour for prep and cooking, and should be allowed to cool for another hour. Once you've piaced your tagine in the oven, put the dessert together and allow it to chill. Lay the appetizers out before the guests arrive. Once they've had their cocktails, your only concerns are taking the tagine out of the oven and the dessert out of the fridge.

Orange-and-Cardamom Martini

Although they don't drink much alcohol in Muslim countries, I took license and created a "Moroccan martini." A couple of things to bear in mind: Always use the best-quality vodka available, and take the time to carefully cut a curlicue or swirl of orange zest to garnish the cocktail. If you like, use orange-flavored vodka.

For a spicier version, you can marinate the cardamom pods and cinnamon sticks in a bottle of vodka beginning at least 24 hours in advance; the spices will infuse the neutral liquor with their heady flavors.

12 ounces vodka
1 1/2 to 2 ounces dry vermouth
6 cardamom pods
6 cinnamon sticks
Zest of 1 orange

1. Chill 6 martini glasses (see page 181).
2. Pour the vodka and vermouth into a shaker filled with ice and shake well. Strain the vodka-vermouth mixture into the chilled glasses, add a cardamom pod and a cinnamon stick to each glass, garnish with the orange zest, and serve.

MARINATED OLIVES AND CHERRY TOMATOES

If you have any leftover ripe tomatoes that you don't want to waste and you're not sure if you want to use them in another salad, here's an excellent use for them.

12 RED CHERRY TOMATOES, WHOLE

12 YELLOW TEARDROP TOMATOES, WHOLE

1 CUP MIXED BLACK AND GREEN OLIVES
(OR ANY COMBINATION YOU FANCY)

½ TEASPOON DRIED RED PEPPER FLAKES
(OR A SMALL AMOUNT OF VERY FINELY MINCED
FRESH CHILI PEPPER)

2 TABLESPOONS OLIVE OIL

1 GARLIC CLOVE, CRUSHED

1 TABLESPOON BALSAMIC VINEGAR

½ TEASPOON COARSE SEA SALT

Combine all the ingredients in a large serving bowl and allow to marinate at room temperature for 1 hour.

OTT

For an additional eye-catching touch, I sprinkled a few bits of edible gold leaf into each cocktail. It's available at Indian markets and at many housewares stores. And don't worry, it's entirely safe as long as you don't consume it in massive quantities.

911

Instead of preparing the appetizers at home, you can buy a wonderful variety of scrumptious specialties in Middle Eastern markets, gourmet delicatessens, and supermarkets. Try baba gannoujh (puréed eggplant salad), dolmades (although they're not Moroccan, these Greek stuffed grape leaves work very well with this menu), all sorts of marinated olives, and tabbouleh (again not Moroccan, but thoroughly compatible with the Middle Eastern theme). Look for a good frozen *pastilla* (*bastila* in Arabic, alternately spelled *b'steeya, bastela,* or *bisteeya*), which is a phyllo-type pastry dough with a filling of squab with almonds, lemon-flavored egg, and spices with a little confectioners' sugar dusted on top. I'd also suggest buying some *cigares,* which are little rolls of pastry filled with an aromatic spicy ground-lamb stuffing. All you have to do is heat them up in the oven or fry them in some vegetable oil.

Hummus

This is one of those recipes that really can't go wrong, and it's great to have extra on hand. It's also nutritious, filling, and healthy. So don't be bashful: Double the recipe and use it for sandwiches, or as a dip or spread. A sandwich of toasted whole-wheat bread and hummus with a salad is a great lunch on the run.

1 15½-ounce can chick peas, drained

1 cup tahini (sesame seed paste)

2 tablespoons plus ¼ cup
freshly squeezed lemon juice
(juice of about 3 lemons)

2 or 3 garlic cloves, crushed

½ teaspoon ground cumin

2 tablespoons chopped fresh flat-leaf parsley

1 teaspoon coarse sea salt

½ teaspoon freshly ground black pepper

1 to 2 teaspoons olive oil, plus ¼ cup

6 small pita breads, cut into wedges

1. In a blender or food processor, combine the chick peas, tahini, lemon juice, garlic, cumin, 1 tablespoon of the parsley, and 6 tablespoons of cold water. Process until the mixture is smooth, adding the additional liquid until the desired consistency is achieved. Season with salt and pepper.
2. Transfer the hummus to a bowl and drizzle with the olive oil. Sprinkle with the remaining tablespoon of parsley and serve with warm or toasted pita bread.

NOTE Hummus can be made a few days in advance and stored in the refrigerator.

Appetizer Buffet

When cocktail hour winds down, you can sit and pass the appetizers around the table or have your guests serve themselves at the buffet. I offer a choice of two recipes that can be served as part of your first-course buffet. You might choose to serve just one, or simply prepare one and buy a prepared version of the other.

I highly recommend serving these appetizers with one or two pockets of warm or toasted pita bread per person. I like to cut the pita into wedges, which are particularly handy for scooping and mopping up. (In fact, the Hummus calls for pita wedges, but you might consider adding an extra bowl of whole pockets or wedges to the table for the other appetizers.)

A Lighter Touch

As an alternative to the pita bread, offer broccoli or cauliflower florets or thin slices of carrot or celery for dipping in the hummus—and indeed in any other dip or spread-type appetizer.

Artichokes Stuffed with Peas

Just before we began work on this book, I traveled to Marrakech and was invited to a dinner party in a private home in the medina. Our host served artichokes and peas, a typical Moroccan dish, simple and delicious—not to mention visually arresting. I was totally inspired and knew right away that I had to reproduce it for my Moroccan-themed party back home. I love the addition of chopped mint, a truly authentic touch.

The great thing about peas is that they are equally good fresh or frozen—and the frozen ones are guaranteed to be 150-watt bright green, since they are picked, frozen, and packed at their peak of freshness.

1 CUP FRESH OR FROZEN PEAS, THAWED IF FROZEN

¼ TEASPOON SALT

⅛ TEASPOON PEPPER

6 MEDIUM TO LARGE ARTICHOKES

1 LEMON, HALVED

3 TABLESPOONS EXTRA-VIRGIN OLIVE OIL

4 SCALLIONS (WHITE AND GREEN PARTS), CHOPPED

1 TABLESPOON PEELED, CHOPPED FRESH GINGER

1 GARLIC CLOVE, FINELY CHOPPED

COARSE SEA SALT AND FRESHLY GROUND
BLACK PEPPER, TO TASTE

¼ CUP PLUS 1 TO 2 TABLESPOONS
COARSELY CHOPPED FRESH MINT

1. Bring a medium pot of salted water to a boil. Blanch the peas in the water for 1 to 2 minutes, drain them in a colander, refresh in cold running water, drain, season with the salt and pepper, and set aside.

2. Bring a large pot of salted water to a boil. Meanwhile, peel the artichokes: Pull the tough outer leaves off by hand and cut the top ½ inch off the tips of the remaining leaves with a small paring knife, leaving the heart and choke. Rub the trimmed artichokes with a lemon half, then place them in the boiling water, cover the pot, and cook over medium heat for 20 to 25 minutes, or until tender (see Note). Remove the artichokes from the pot, drain, and allow to cool enough to handle before removing the choke with a spoon. Set aside.

3. Place the oil in a frying pan over medium heat. Add the scallions, ginger, and garlic, and sauté for 1 minute. Add the blanched peas, season with salt and pepper, and cook for an additional 1 to 2 minutes, until the peas are warm. Add ¼ cup of the mint, mix well, and remove from heat.

4. Spoon the pea mixture into the artichoke hearts, arrange on a platter, garnish with the remaining chopped mint, and serve warm.

NOTE To test artichokes for doneness, remove one from the pot and pierce its heart with a paring knife. If the knife slides in easily, it's done. Alternatively, pull on a leaf and if it comes off easily, it's done. The artichokes can be prepared in advance and reheated before being stuffed. Simply place them in an ovenproof glass dish in a 350°F. oven until warm, about 10 minutes. If an artichoke won't stand up on a flat surface, slice off a small portion of the bottom to flatten it.

911

Use canned artichoke hearts, which are precooked. Simply heat them in the microwave, skip step 2 of the recipe, and proceed with step 3.

Tagine of Chicken

This is a simplified tagine, a one-pot dish with elegant, subtle flavors that are aromatic-spicy (as opposed to hot-spicy). Its most distinctive flavor notes are the saffron and the lovely hints of citrus that come from the preserved lemons. I took creative license by adding some wine to the recipe. The melding of flavors is indescribably delicious. The chicken is cooked in a heavy-bottom pot and presented at the table in a tagine (see 411, next page). Glazed tagines have a high likelihood of lead content, so unless you're sure that yours is lead-free, cook in a safe pan and use the tagine for serving only.

2 WHOLE CHICKENS (ABOUT 4 POUNDS EACH),
BACKS REMOVED, EACH CUT INTO 8 PIECES

2 BREASTS OF CHICKEN, BONE IN, HALVED

1 TABLESPOON COARSE SEA SALT

1 TEASPOON FRESHLY GROUND BLACK PEPPER

4 TABLESPOONS OLIVE OIL

2 TABLESPOONS UNSALTED BUTTER

1 1/2 TEASPOONS GROUND CUMIN

1 1/2 TEASPOONS GROUND GINGER

1 1/2 TEASPOONS SWEET PAPRIKA

1 TEASPOON FRESH SAFFRON THREADS

JUICE OF 1 LEMON

2 GARLIC CLOVES, FINELY MINCED

1/2 CUP WHITE WINE

1 1/2 CUPS CHICKEN STOCK (PAGE 120)

1 CUP PITTED GREEN OR PURPLE OLIVES
(IF HARD, BLANCH IN BOILING WATER FOR 2 MINUTES,
OR UNTIL TENDER)

2 PRESERVED LEMONS (SEE PAGE 94),
CUT INTO 1/4-INCH DICE

1 TABLESPOON CHOPPED FRESH FLAT-LEAF PARSLEY

1 TABLESPOON CHOPPED FRESH CILANTRO

1. Preheat the oven to 350°F.

2. Season the whole chicken and breasts with the salt and pepper. Place the oil in a large ovenproof skillet or Dutch oven over medium-high heat. Add the chicken in batches (don't crowd the pan) and brown on all sides, about 5 minutes each batch.

3. When all the chicken is browned, remove the excess fat from the skillet and return all of the chicken pieces to the skillet. Add the butter, cumin, ginger, paprika, saffron, lemon juice, garlic, white wine, and stock and bring to a boil. Cover the skillet, place in the oven, and bake for 30 minutes. Add the olives and lemons, basting and turning the chicken. Leave the skillet uncovered, and bake for an additional 10 minutes.

4. Transfer the contents of the skillet to the tagine, sprinkle with parsley and cilantro, and serve immediately with the couscous (see page 83) on the side. Open the top ceremoniously at the table . . . if you like.

411: Tagine

Like the Spanish paella, *tagine* refers to both the cooking vessel and the dish that emerges from it. It is Morocco's world-wide gastronomic ambassador; if you haven't heard of tagine with couscous, then you haven't heard of Moroccan cuisine. A tagine is a wide, low, circular terra-cotta baking dish that has a conical cover with a knobby handle on top. Traditionally, tagines are placed on the stove, and the ingredients are simmered over very low heat; they can also be cooked in the oven. Typically, they contain various marinated, spiced ingredients—vegetables, lamb, chicken, seafood. Chicken with lemons and olives is a staple.

Decorative or ceremonial tagines are used only for serving; the dish is prepared first in a skillet or Dutch oven–type pan, as is the case in this recipe. A traditional tagine for cooking has an unglazed interior, which causes the steam and cooking liquids to gradually reduce and concentrate as the dish slowly simmers.

Moroccan Tomato and Eggplant Salad

This is a savory, moist salad, like a purée of ratatouille, featuring strong notes of cumin and a little bite from the hot chili flakes. The recipe suggests serving it with pita bread. Another option is to place lettuce cups on salad plates, fill them with the eggplant mixture, and serve it as a first course. Or simply serve with carrot sticks.

1 LARGE EGGPLANT, HALVED LENGTHWISE
3 TABLESPOONS EXTRA-VIRGIN OLIVE OIL,
PLUS ADDITIONAL FOR GARNISH
4 LARGE TOMATOES, COARSELY CHOPPED
4 GARLIC CLOVES, FINELY MINCED
5 TABLESPOONS TOMATO PASTE
1/2 TEASPOON DRIED RED PEPPER FLAKES
2 TABLESPOONS GROUND CUMIN
COARSE SEA SALT AND FRESHLY GROUND
BLACK PEPPER, TO TASTE
WARM TOASTED PITA BREAD, FOR SERVING

1. Preheat the oven to 325°F.
2. Brush the eggplant halves with 2 tablespoons of the olive oil and place them skin side down on a baking sheet. Bake the eggplant in the oven for 1 hour, or until its flesh is tender. Remove it from the oven and allow to cool.
3. Scoop the pulp from the eggplant, discard the seeds and skin, chop the pulp fine, and set aside.
4. Place the remaining tablespoon of olive oil, the tomatoes, garlic, tomato paste, and pepper flakes in a large skillet over medium heat. Cook for 5 minutes, stirring occasionally. Add the chopped eggplant and cumin, and blend well. Continue to cook over low heat for 30 minutes, or until most of the liquid has evaporated. Season with salt and pepper.
5. To serve, place in a bowl, sprinkle with extra-virgin olive oil to taste, and accompany with warm toasted pita bread.

NOTE This salad should be served warm or at room temperature, so allow about 20 minutes for it to cool after removing from the heat. If it's made in advance, remove it from the fridge at least an hour before serving.

Rosewater-Scented Towels

In summer, add ¼ cup rosewater to 1½ cups cold water. Douse hand towels in the rosewater-scented water, wring out the excess, place the towels in a dish, and leave them in the freezer while you're having cocktails. In winter, place the same towels in a glass ovenproof dish, cover the dish, and microwave on high for 5 minutes. Rosewater, by the way, is the distilled essence of rose petals. It has been a common flavoring ingredient in Asian and Middle Eastern cuisines for thousands of years.

OTT

- Burn some incense in the living room or powder room.
- On a hot balmy evening, give each of your guests a chilled rosewater-scented towel to wipe their hands before commencing dinner.
- It's considered polite to eat a lot of this food with your hands. So be my guest!

411: Couscous

Couscous is granular semolina, the same flour of coarsely ground durum wheat that is used to make fine pastas. It can also refer to both the preparation and the cooking vessel in which it is prepared—a kind of steamer that holds the pasta on top while meats and other savory ingredients simmer below. Across northern Africa, there are numerous variations of the recipe. The couscous we buy in the market is precooked, so just follow the directions on the package.

COUSCOUS WITH DRIED FRUITS AND WALNUTS

Couscous and tagine are the pasta and tomato sauce of Moroccan cuisine, a natural and ubiquitous pairing. Couscous, by the way, is an ideal light starch accompaniment for many entrées. By adding golden raisins, dried apricots and dates, and toasted almonds, you can take a plain version of this dish and make it both extra colorful and extra tasty. On the plate, the couscous absorbs the wonderful cooking juices from the chicken, and its dried fruits are an excellent foil for the spices in the tagine.

2 CUPS PRECOOKED DRIED COUSCOUS

1/4 CUP FINELY CHOPPED DATES

1/4 CUP GOLDEN RAISINS

1/4 CUP CUBED DRIED APRICOTS

1/4 CUP TOASTED ALMOND SLIVERS

1 TABLESPOON UNSALTED BUTTER

1 TEASPOON SALT

In a large bowl, mix the couscous with the dates, raisins, apricots, almonds, butter, and salt. Cook the mixture according to the directions on the couscous package. (The rule of thumb is 2 cups of liquid for every 1 cup of couscous.) When the couscous is done, fluff it with a fork, transfer to a platter, and serve alongside the tagine.

A Quick Moroccan Primer

Djellabah: A big kaftan for men in cotton or silk; they are often beautifully embroidered.

Fez: The traditional Arab dressy hat—red and cylindrical with a black tassel.

Henna: A paste made from the dried leaves of the Egyptian privet, used to decorate brides' hands and feet with beautiful, intricate designs ("temporary tattoos"); also for hair conditioning and coloring.

Kesra: An anise-scented bread used to scoop up food from a communal dish.

Marhaba: "Welcome."

Medina: The old city center.

Mezze: Multiple bowls of appetizers.

Rashasha: A dispenser or sprinkler for perfumed waters with a bulbous shape and long stem.

Souk: The central marketplace or bazaar, a maze of buildings and small partially covered streets that are arranged in a surprisingly consistent and carefully planned manner throughout the Arab world.

Touma: Garlic.

Ward: Rosewater.

Zaater: Oregano.

Zahar: Orange-blossom water.

411: Orange-Blossom Water

Also known as orange-flower water (and *zahar* in Morocco), this is the distilled essence of the flowers of bitter (or Seville) oranges. It is used to flavor drinks, pastries, and candies. You'll find it in most Middle Eastern markets, stored on the shelf in its sealed bottle or jar.

STRAWBERRIES AND ORANGE SLICES IN ORANGE-BLOSSOM WATER WITH MINT

After we've all shared our marvelous memories of Morocco amid much other merriment, we conclude our souk soirée with a typical dessert of chilled fresh fruit marinated with cinnamon, sugar, mint, and orange-blossom water. It's the easiest dessert in the world to make, and it's guaranteed to cleanse the palate, leaving a clean, fresh impression to go with fond memories of a remarkable meal.

4 NAVEL ORANGES, PEELED AND CUT INTO CUBES

1 POUND STRAWBERRIES,
STEMS REMOVED, CLEANED, DRIED, AND QUARTERED

1 CINNAMON STICK

1 TABLESPOON ORANGE-BLOSSOM WATER
(OR ESSENCE OF ORANGE)

2 TABLESPOONS SUGAR

¼ CUP COARSELY CHOPPED FRESH MINT

Combine all the ingredients in a bowl and mix well. Allow to chill for at least 1 hour before serving.

MINT TEA

A soothing, relaxing herbal tea is the perfect finale to this supper. Make your favorite Jasmine tea or other similar black tea. Add liberal portions of chopped mint and granulated sugar, and allow the tea to steep for 5 to 10 minutes. Serve hot.

PERI-PERI—CHA! CHA! CHA!
FOR 4

We all got dressed up for a night on the town, but of course you can't party on an empty stomach. So I decided to make a chic little supper, which I served in my living room. And judging by the way my guests were dressed, I'm happy I dressed my table.

We started off the evening on the right note with saketinis, an exciting cocktail I discovered at Bond Street, one of the trendier restaurants on the downtown Manhattan scene. Serving a novelty cocktail is always a great way to jump-start the evening.

At the cocktail area, I placed a single large chartreuse cymbidium orchid stem in a simple sculptural vase. With its thick shaft and multiple blossoms, a single stem makes a bold, elegant statement. These flowers are readily available in the corner market when they're in season, and they last a week or so.

The table setting featured Japanese lacquer trays with pairs of diamond-shaped black and burgundy candles standing guard at each setting. I really favor these big, sturdy types of candle; not only are they long-lasting, clean, and efficient, but they can be visually interesting. I created an eye-catching centerpiece from a concertina of test tubes, an intriguing and slightly offbeat item that you find in specialty stores. Rather than filling them with the predictable cut flowers, I created a hedge of curly parsley. To crown it all, I positioned a sculpture of an Indian brave by the Austrian sculptor Hagenauer in the center of the parsley.

Instead of a hedge of parsley, which by the way is extremely doable, you might choose to create a lineup of your favorite flowers. It could be poppies in springtime, or perhaps miniature black calla lilies or black cosmos flowers, each in its own tube. Alternatively, consider using another grocery-store item such as mint.

When it came time for dinner, I served the mussels to each guest—always a gracious touch. For the main course, both the chicken and the rice are arranged on platters and passed around. The food itself has an exotic Afro-Portuguese touch with the mussels in coconut milk and the stewed chicken, two dishes that are deceptively simple given how much flavor they offer. Most importantly, it's all sexy and spicy and not too heavy.

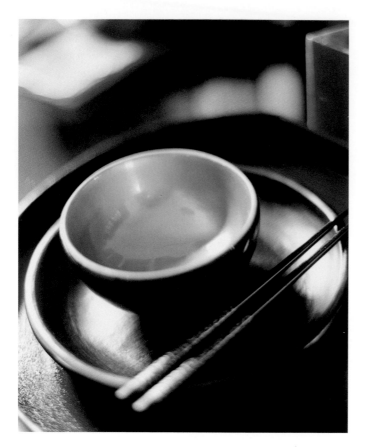

411: Lacquer

Lacquer is an ancient decorative art that began in China at least 2,000 years ago. It was subsequently exported to Korea and then Japan, where it became prevalent in the seventh century A.D. It was also adopted in Europe beginning in the seventeenth century.

To create traditional lacquer, skilled craftsmen applied many layers of a varnish usually made from the resins of a type of tree in the sumac family. Fine lacquer would receive up to forty coats, each of which was dried, smoothed, and polished by hand. Modern lacquers made from synthetic materials are used to coat everything from cars to furniture. Lacquer can be inlaid with shells or precious metals, particularly gold. Among the antique items made from lacquer are eating and writing utensils, storage boxes and cases, ceremonial vessels, and sword scabbards. Authentic antique lacquer is expensive and rare; most of it is to be found in museums. Modern imitations are easy to find, inexpensive, durable, practical, and *très* chic.

TABLE SETTINGS

Some people get their thrills from bungee jumping or scuba diving to two hundred feet; others have a penchant for expensive jewelry. One of mine is setting tables.

It used to be we set tables according to etiquette books, and there wasn't much room for individual expression. But table arrangements can really offer a window into a person's soul. The effort we make dressing up our homes and tables, how much trouble we've taken to make our guests feel welcome, how creative and resourceful we've been—all are wonderful forms of projecting character.

In planning a table setting, I always try to come up with some sort of eye-catching centerpiece. The vast majority of party-givers resort to expensive vases and the lavish use of cut flowers. I much prefer to work with a few simple elements, selected for harmony and arranged with a sense of sensuality, to create something that belongs in that space.

Always look to exercise your creativity and put a different spin on things. Everyone's edge is different; try finding yours. For table settings, one of my favorite approaches is to think outside the box while at the same time incorporating everyday objects. For example, the multiple test-tube holder filled with parsley, a common grocery item: It's an elegant, evocative, clever way to dress up your table. Better yet, it's simple and unpretentious. Fresh-cut roses would have cost a lot and would not have made a better impression. (Don't get me wrong, roses are beautiful. But really, how clever or original are they?) A parsley centerpiece using a multiple test-tube holder—now that's something new and different!

The Menu: Supper for Four

Appetizer
Curried Mussels in Coconut-Milk Broth
with Lemongrass

Main Course
Peri-Peri Chicken
Savory Basmati Rice

Dessert
Orange Custard Tart

To Drink
Cocktail de Nuit: Saketini

White Wine
A good oaky Chardonnay will stand up well to the spices in
the curried mussels and the Peri-Peri chicken.
A well-chilled Alsatian Gewürztraminer or Pinot Gris
(Trimbach is a fine producer) would also fit the bill. Ditto a
German Riesling with some residual sugar to
balance the spices and some clean acidity to
complement the richness of the coconut broth.

TIMING The orange tart should be made in advance—the night
before would be ideal. The chicken takes a minimum of 2 hours
to marinate, so get it ready before you jump in the shower. When
the guests arrive, the chicken goes in the oven and the rice goes
in the cooker. The mussels take about 15 minutes to cook, so as
the host you'll disappear for that period of time toward the end of
the cocktail interlude. Seat your guests when the mussels have
begun to steam open and serve them right out of the pot. You
can take the chicken out of the oven just before serving the mussels, and leave it covered on the stove. It stays plenty hot and
gives you time to enjoy the first course. If you plan to make the
chicken in advance, allow 20 to 25 minutes for it to reheat in the
oven. Party time is 2 hours or less—45 minutes to 1 hour for
cocktails, and 1 hour for dinner—which is why this is the ideal
launch for a night on the town.

OTT
Serve an ounce (about 2 spoons)
of caviar on a mother-of-pearl
spoon with each saketini as an
amuse-bouche. As a garnish for
the martini, sprinkle some edible
gold-leaf flakes on top, available
at Indian markets and houseware stores (see Resources).

Saketini

The saketini can actually be made with either sake (rice wine)
or plum wine, whichever you prefer or whichever is more readily
available. With the surging popularity of Japanese cuisine, you
shouldn't have trouble finding either at your local wine merchant
or liquor store.

4 ounces high-quality lemon-infused vodka
8 ounces sake or plum wine
Splash of cranberry juice
Splash of grapefruit juice
2 to 3 drops of Triple Sec
1 lime, cut into wedges or slices, for garnish

1. Chill 4 martini glasses (see page 181).
2. Pour all the liquid ingredients into a shaker full of ice. Shake
vigorously, strain into the glasses, and garnish with a small
wedge or slice of lime to serve.

CURRIED MUSSELS IN COCONUT-MILK BROTH WITH LEMONGRASS

This is the simplest and most delectable of recipes. Mussels are inexpensive and relatively easy to prepare, but very special to serve. If you follow a multi-step French-style recipe, this type of dish could become quite complicated. You might be dirtying four or five pots, shelling the mussels, reducing the broth, whisking in thickener. This is easier. Here, all you do is combine the ingredients in one pot and steam open the mussels.

What about eating utensils? Nature always provides. When eating mussels, it's not necessary to use a fork, spoon, or even the chopsticks that were set on the table for this dinner. Simply pluck the meat out of the shells using another empty shell as a pincer. Be sure to serve the mussels with a good crusty bread to soak up all the delicious broth.

I TABLESPOON UNSALTED BUTTER

I SHALLOT, FINELY CHOPPED

I TABLESPOON CURRY POWDER

¼ CUP DRY WHITE WINE

I CUP COCONUT MILK

I LEMONGRASS STALK, CUT INTO 4 PIECES

2 POUNDS (MEDIUM SIZE) BLACK MUSSELS,
BEARDS REMOVED, WASHED, AND DRAINED

I TEASPOON COARSE SEA SALT, PLUS MORE TO TASTE

½ TEASPOON FRESHLY GROUND BLACK PEPPER,
PLUS MORE TO TASTE

1. Melt the butter over medium heat in a pot large enough to hold all the mussels. Add the shallot and cook 1 minute (see Note), or until soft. Add the curry powder, wine, coconut milk, and lemongrass and cook for 3 minutes.

2. Add the mussels and stir well. Increase the heat to high and cover the pot. Cook for 5 to 8 minutes, or until all mussels have opened. (Remove and discard any that don't open.) Season with salt and pepper. Transfer equal portions of the mussels and their liquid to bowls and serve.

NOTE Always cook mussels on the day you purchase them. Never pry open a cooked mollusk. If it hasn't opened on its own, it is not meant to be eaten.

Variation

Substitute littleneck or Manila clams for the mussels.

Peri-Peri Chicken

Here's one of my all-time favorites, a fiery Portuguese chicken dish that was a staple where I grew up in southern Africa. It's based on a rather exotic spicy sauce, Perks Peri-Peri African Heat (see Shopping Resources). I have a soft spot in my heart for Peri-Peri—it reminds me of my roots—and I usually buy a case of it at a time. It's one of those amazingly versatile items that I like to have around for spontaneous cooking inspiration.

This recipe includes Portuguese spice, Lebanese olives, and Moroccan preserved lemon I added after a trip there—a delightful co-mingling of cultures, truly global fusion cuisine. Another thing I love about this preparation: While it's definitely not your run-of-the-mill chicken stew, it's in and out of the oven in no more than an hour, which makes it ideal for the busy host who wants to give his or her guests the attention they deserve. I recommend making an extra-large batch since it's just as great the next day.

The amount of hot sauce may be adjusted according to its strength and your personal preference. This dish can be prepared without the lemon, olives, or garlic, but each of them adds a new flavor note.

I WHOLE CHICKEN
(ABOUT 4 POUNDS), WASHED, PATTED DRY,
BACK REMOVED, TRIMMED OF EXCESS FAT AND SKIN,
AND CUT INTO 8 PIECES

I CUP PERI-PERI SAUCE
(OR ANY EQUIVALENT HOT PEPPER SAUCE; ADJUST AMOUNT
ACCORDING TO TASTE)

8 GARLIC CLOVES LEFT WHOLE

I TABLESPOON COARSE SEA SALT

1/2 TABLESPOON FRESHLY GROUND BLACK PEPPER

I 2 GREEN OLIVES
(OR BLACK ONES, IF YOU PREFER; PITTING THEM IS OPTIONAL)

I PRESERVED LEMON (RECIPE FOLLOWS),
PULP REMOVED, BLANCHED, PEELED, AND COARSELY CHOPPED

2 LEMONS,
CUT INTO WEDGES FOR GARNISH AND SQUEEZING

1. Place the chicken skin side up in an ovenproof glass dish just large enough to hold all the pieces in a single layer. Pour the sauce over the chicken, cover the dish with plastic wrap, and place in the refrigerator to marinate for 2 hours or more. The longer it marinates, the hotter the chicken. (For cooking, it's important that the chicken pieces be arranged with no space between them. Using a dish that is too large will cause the sauce to burn off when cooking.)
2. Preheat the oven to 450°F.

(continued on page 94)

411: Peri-Peri

Peri-peri is a chili bean that was introduced to Africa by Portuguese spice traders about 400 years ago. The spice mixture based on peri-peri chilies is one of the staples of South African cuisine and a key ingredient in my preferred hot sauce, Perks Peri-Peri African Heat, which is very spicy indeed. The wonderful thing about this sauce, though, is that the chili's heat is not long-lasting: It gives you a good burn up front and then it subsides gracefully, thanks to the subtlety and complexity of the peri-peri mix. Any well-conceived, high-quality prepared hot sauce will share the same qualities and is an acceptable substitute.

3. Bring 2 cups of water to a boil in a small saucepan. Add the garlic cloves and cook over medium heat for 10 minutes. Drain the cloves and place them in the dish under the chicken. Season the chicken with the salt and pepper. Bake for 50 minutes skin side up, basting every 15 minutes.

4. After 50 minutes, remove the dish from the oven and increase the heat to broil. Add the olives and preserved lemon to the dish. Baste the chicken, then place it skin side up under the broiler for an additional 5 to 10 minutes, or until the skin becomes crispy.

5. Remove the chicken from the oven, cover the dish lightly with aluminum foil, and allow the chicken to rest for up to 15 minutes as you complete your first course. To serve, transfer the chicken to a platter along with fresh quartered lemons. A few dashes of fresh lemon juice help balance all the flavors and cut the bite of the hot marinade.

Preserved Lemons

To use these lemons, scrape away the seeds and the remnants of the flesh, and use only the skins. Before using, blanch them in boiling water for up to 1 minute to remove any bitterness.

Preserved lemons can be stored in a tight jar in the fridge for up to 6 months. I like to make them at least a month in advance of use. They can also be found in most Middle Eastern markets and can be used in many recipes, including Moroccan tagines (page 81). They are also excellent with marinated olives, in salads, or with broiled or grilled fish.

ENOUGH LEMONS TO FILL A SEALABLE JAR
OF YOUR CHOOSING

COARSE SEA SALT

ENOUGH VEGETABLE OIL TO COVER ALL THE LEMONS

1. Wash the lemons under cold running water, then pat them dry.

2. Cut a small slice off the bottom of each lemon so it can stand upright. With the lemon standing upright, make two diametrical cuts at a 90-degree angle to each other about two thirds of the way down through the lemon as if you were going to cut it into quarters; do not cut all the way through.

3. Squeeze the cuts open and fill each lemon with about 1 tablespoon of the salt.

4. Pack the lemons tightly into the jar. Fill the jar completely with the vegetable oil, seal it, and refrigerate for 1 month.

SAVORY BASMATI RICE

I highly recommend you cook this dish with a rice cooker, which is well worth the investment. The cooker stops when the rice is done and keeps it warm until ready to serve. If you do use the cooker, simply sauté the vegetables in a separate skillet until soft, then transfer to the rice cooker, add the rice and stock, stir, and follow the instructions that come with the cooker.

1 TABLESPOON UNSALTED BUTTER

1 GARLIC CLOVE, CRUSHED

1 MEDIUM YELLOW ONION, CHOPPED (ABOUT 1/2 CUP)

1/4 TEASPOON GROUND TURMERIC

1 CUP WHITE BASMATI RICE, RINSED

1 CUP CHICKEN STOCK (PAGE 120)

1/2 TEASPOON SALT

1 CINNAMON STICK

1. Melt the butter in a large skillet over medium-low heat. Reduce the heat to low; add the garlic, onion, and turmeric. Cook uncovered for 10 minutes.

2. Add the rice, stock, salt, and cinnamon. Stir well to coat the rice and distribute the flavors. Bring to a boil, then reduce the heat to low, cover, and cook for 20 minutes, or until all the liquid is absorbed.

3. Remove from the heat, but keep covered for 5 minutes. Fluff with a fork, discard the cinnamon, and arrange on a platter.

411: Cooking Rice

For every cup of rice, use a cup of liquid (water, stock, wine, or a combination) and add 1/2 teaspoon of salt. Keep these proportions regardless of quantities. But remember that the rice will nearly double in size when cooked, so don't fill a pot to the top with raw rice and water. Allow room for the rice to expand, and for you to be able to fluff the cooked rice without it spilling onto your counters and floor.

Orange Custard Tart

Although this tart is easy to prepare, it can be time-consuming. So don't be bashful about skipping this recipe if time is short and simply buying dessert. I would recommend something refreshing and light: say, a fruit-and-sorbet concoction along the lines of the desserts in "Dirty Movies" (page 200). Or keep it simple with just a scoop or two of orange and/or mango sorbet. When you have time, try this recipe. It's a lot of fun, it's not complex, and it's very impressive.

FOR THE SWEET DOUGH

1 1/2 CUPS FLOUR

1/4 CUP CONFECTIONERS' SUGAR

4 OUNCES (1 STICK) UNSALTED BUTTER, COLD, CUT INTO SMALL CUBES

1 LARGE EGG

FOR THE CUSTARD FILLING

12 OUNCES (3 STICKS) UNSALTED BUTTER, CUT INTO PIECES

1 CUP PLUS 2 TABLESPOONS ORANGE JUICE

ZEST OF 4 ORANGES

5 LARGE EGGS

1 CUP SUGAR

FOR THE GARNISH

1 RECIPE ORANGE GARNISH (RECIPE FOLLOWS)

1. Prepare the dough: Place the flour, confectioners' sugar, and butter in a food processor and pulse until well combined and the texture of small crumbs. Add the egg and continue to pulse until firm enough to form a ball of dough. Form the ball, wrap it in plastic, and place in the refrigerator for 30 minutes.

2. Preheat the oven to 350°F.

3. Grease a 13 × 4-inch rectangular pastry mold with butter. (Alternatively, you can use a round mold 9 or 10 inches in diameter.) On a lightly floured surface, roll out the dough to a thickness of 1/4 inch and press it into the pastry mold. Score the dough all over with a fork. Lay parchment paper on top of the dough and weight it with about 1 pound of uncooked beans or rice. Place the mold on a baking sheet and bake for 15 to 20 minutes, or

until lightly browned. Remove from the oven and allow to cool at room temperature.

4. Prepare the filling: Mix all the custard ingredients except the eggs and half the sugar together in a large bowl and then transfer to a saucepan over medium heat. Stir until the mixture is warm and the butter is melted. Remove from the heat immediately. In another bowl, beat the eggs and the remaining 1/2 cup sugar until smooth. Gradually add the warm butter mixture from the pan, beating constantly. Then place the entire filling mixture back in the saucepan over medium flame and heat until it just bubbles. (Do not overheat or you will get scrambled eggs.)

5. Place the mixture in a blender and pulse one or two times, until smooth. Fill the pastry shell with the custard mixture and refrigerate until the filling is set and the tart is cold, at least 1 hour.

6. To serve, arrange slices of orange garnish in overlapping fashion like fish scales, or in any other pattern you fancy.

Orange Garnish

This orange garnish can be made 2 to 3 days in advance and stored in a covered glass container in the refrigerator. Extra slices can be used to garnish other desserts including sorbet, fruit salad, and chocolate mousse.

1 CUP SUGAR

1 ORANGE, WASHED, HALVED, SEEDS REMOVED, AND THINLY SLICED

1. Place the sugar and 2 cups of water in a medium saucepan over medium-low heat. Add the orange slices and simmer for 30 to 40 minutes, until the orange slices are soft but not mushy; they should retain their shape.

2. Set the orange slices and their syrup aside to cool, then refrigerate until ready to use.

AFRICA, MY HOME
FOR 6

It is a midsummer weekend, and I am invited to be a houseguest at the lovely East Hampton home of my good friends Kai and Doron Linz and their children. Doron and I both grew up in southern Africa, and the couple commissioned me to design and plan their wedding, which is what cemented our friendship.

On the East Coast, the Hamptons are the closest thing we have to California. The climate is a bit damper, but the light, the scenery, the lifestyle, the freedom to express one's personal style and enjoy the outdoors to its fullest are all quite similar.

When I'm a guest, if my hosts are willing—and they usually are—I like to plan a dinner party one night during the weekend. Since Doron and I share the African upbringing, I felt this was the clear choice for the evening's theme. The Horn of Africa is a crossroads of world cultures and cuisines. Durban and the Port of Cape Town were a major stopping-off point on the Spice Route between America, Europe, and the Far East. Consequently, Cape Malay cuisine absorbed all the influences of Portuguese, Malaysian, Indian, Indonesian, and other Far Eastern schools of cooking.

Traditionally, the finer cuts of meat were reserved for the privileged and the upper classes while the working people and the poor had to make do with the rest. Ever resourceful, the people of Cape Malay made delicious long-cooked stews with the tougher, bonier cuts such as shoulder, tail, leg, and knuckle of various livestock.

Our main course for the evening is traditionally prepared in a *potjie* (pronounced "poy-kee"), which is Afrikaans for a cast-iron pot. (I still have mine and use it regularly.) As with couscous and tagine, the vessel and the dish are often referred to by the same term. The cooking method is to fill one of these with meat, vegetables, herbs, spices, and other aromatic ingredients, set it directly on top of a bed of hot coals, and let it slowly bubble away for three to six hours or more. This yields a mouth-watering stew that, on top of a bed of rice, can feed a very large extended family. I don't think there's anyone who grew up in southern Africa who doesn't have fond memories of these hearty stews, and this is exactly the dish for our outdoor Hamptons dinner.

The trading routes encompassed so many cultures with so much to offer in cuisine and decor. I try to reflect that in our table arrangement. The tablecloth is a West African kente cloth, woven into a beautiful geometrical pattern with the typical stripes and bars,

Cultivating an International Style

I grew up in southern Africa, emigrated to the United States with its multiple cultures, and have spent the better part of my adult formative years living in Los Angeles and New York, two global crossroads. I like to embrace what all the cultures of the world have to offer in terms of cuisine, decor, and ambience. I suppose you could call it eclecticism, but I'm wary of that label because over the past couple of decades I think it came to represent a kind of carelessness or thoughtlessness in design and decorating. Let's try some synonyms: broad, wide-ranging, all-embracing, diverse, heterogeneous, inclusive, universal.

My cooking philosophy falls in line with my overall decorating and entertaining aesthetic. I like to use a broad palette, to assimilate as many interesting flavors from as many national and regional cuisines as possible. Then I adapt the recipes, streamlining them without sacrificing one bit of flavor or excitement. If you can cook a dish in three steps within an hour that traditionally takes seven or eight steps and three hours—and without losing its edge—then by all means do it.

which is traditionally draped over the shoulders as part of ceremonial dress. The table setting also features cast-iron flatware from Thailand; Indonesian woven-straw brass-rimmed chargers; hand-crafted Chinese pottery serving plates; and hand-painted ceramic monkey-design plates from Portugal. You'd very likely encounter objects from any and all of these countries in a home in southern Africa. Nowadays in the United States we're discovering many corners of the globe, like the one where I grew up, places where the cross-pollination of cultures has created beautiful arts and crafts and delectable cuisines.

Africa is all about feast and famine, death and procreation. The spiritual and the mundane, the profound and the quotidian, are continually juxtaposed on a daily basis. I try to reflect this phenomenon in the table arrangement. Corn having been the staple of the African diet for centuries, I feature it not only in the appetizer course but in the centerpiece for the table. No need for cut flowers if you can create an eye-catching piece with a common grocery item like this and a few strategically placed candles.

The table and buffet layouts may look complicated, but they're not. They take literally fifteen minutes to set up; the trick was that I'd taken the time, over a period of years, to assemble all the objects. But that's the fun part: If you're someone who likes to entertain, anytime you go shopping, keep an eye out for items that might enhance your tabletop arrangements.

The Menu: Supper for Six

Appetizer
Maize Fritters with Garlic Aïoli

Main Course
Tomato Lamb Bredie
Aromatic Basmati Rice
Tomato Sambal
Peach Chutney

Dessert
Cape Brandy Tart with Brandy Sauce

To Drink
Cocktail de Nuit: Ponana Souk

Wine: Merlot
Try a nice, rounded, medium- to full-bodied Merlot or
Merlot-based wine. My choice for the evening was the 1989
Meelust Merlot from the Stellenbosch region of South
Africa. Since the end of apartheid and the lifting
of sanctions, connoisseurs the world over have been
discovering the excellent wines of South Africa. I brought
a couple of magnums of this one back with me on my last
trip. It pairs extremely well with the lamb stew.

TIMING The dough for the fritters should be prepared in
advance. The fritters can also be fried in advance, then reheated
in the oven or the microwave; or they can be fried at the end of
the cocktail hour, drained, then served immediately. The lamb
stew should be simmering in its pot by the time the guests
arrive. The tomato salad can be prepared in advance and
allowed to marinate in its dressing. The chutney can be prepared in advance or store-bought. The brandy tart can be made
in advance and even frozen.

Ponana Souk

This is a potent, refreshing, and memorable cocktail. The Amaretto gives it just a hint of that inimitable bittersweet almond flavor. It is my version of a drink I first encountered at the Ponana Souk, which was one of Los Angeles's greatest nightclubs some years ago. As I recall, they used to down it as shots there. But I've made it much more palatable here by pouring it over ice.

2½ to 3 ounces Amaretto liqueur
10 to 12 ounces vodka
10 to 12 ounces peach schnapps
10 to 12 ounces cranberry juice
10 to 12 ounces pineapple juice
6 sprigs fresh mint, for garnish

Pour all the ingredients into a pitcher and stir. Divide among 6 rocks glasses over ice with a sprig of fresh mint in each glass.

Maize Fritters with Garlic Aïoli

Corn is a major staple of the African diet; likewise, fritters are ubiquitous. So nothing could remind me more of home than these crispy nuggets. By using a light oil for frying and by draining them properly, you guarantee they will turn out light and ever-so-tasty. The teaspoon-size dollops of dough, when placed in the hot oil, will expand and become quite light and fluffy due to the addition of baking powder. Although the recipe has been simplified and adapted, and is made from Cream of Wheat rather than cornmeal, these fritters replicate the corn flavor as I remember it extremely well.

2 cups (2 servings) Cream of Wheat
(or other hot wheat cereal)

2 cups cake flour

2 teaspoons baking powder

2 cups grated Cheddar cheese
(about ½ pound)

2 eggs, beaten

1 tablespoon powdered chicken bouillon

1 tablespoon fine salt, plus more to taste

¼ teaspoon chili powder

Vegetable oil, to fill your pot halfway

1 recipe Garlic Aïoli (recipe follows)

1. Prepare the Cream of Wheat according to the instructions on the box. Set aside and allow to cool.

2. In a large bowl, combine the flour, baking powder, cheese, eggs, the powdered bouillon, half the salt, the chili powder, and the porridge; mix well to form a fairly smooth batter. If necessary, add a small amount of milk to thin it.

3. Fill a cast-iron pot, wok, or other deep-frying pan halfway to the top with vegetable oil. Place the pot over medium-high heat until the oil reaches a temperature of 375°F. (see 411). When the oil is ready, use a teaspoon to scoop dollops of batter about 1 inch in diameter out of the bowl. Using a slotted spoon, carefully slide them into the hot oil, one by one, and fry them until they are golden brown and floating, about 2 minutes. Turn the fritters often in order to brown them evenly. Remove them to a platter lined with paper towel to drain. Sprinkle with the remaining salt and the chili powder while they're still hot, and serve with Garlic Aïoli for dipping. Alternatively, fry them in advance, set aside at room temperature after draining, and reheat in the microwave on high for 25 to 40 seconds, or in a preheated 350°F. oven for 5 to 10 minutes.

411: Gauging the Temperature of Frying Oil

If you plan to do any deep frying, it's important to correctly gauge the temperature of your oil. You don't want it to be too hot, to the point where it burns your food, making it taste bitter, but it should be hot enough to harden and caramelize the exterior so that the interior cooks quickly without absorbing the oil and hence turning your dish soggy. The best way to measure the temperature of hot oil is with a candy thermometer, which measures the higher temperatures needed for melting and hardening in candy recipes. Candy thermometers are available in most cookware and houseware stores and are a good investment if you plan to do any deep-frying (or of course if you plan to make candy). If you don't have one, drop a small piece of bread in the hot oil. If it turns brown quickly, the oil is ready. Alternatively, throw a drop of water in; if it sizzles immediately, you can start frying.

Although some recipes call for frying foods in oil that has just reached its smoking point, in general if the oil is smoking it's too hot for proper deep-frying. Most foods are deep-fried at temperatures in the 350° to 375°F. range. The larger the piece of food, the lower the temperature within this range, since the interior of the piece needs more time to become done. If a piece of food sinks right to the bottom of the oil and doesn't rise, then the oil is definitely not hot enough for frying. (That's why it's always important to test first.) If the oil isn't hot enough, the food will become soggy and drenched with oil; if it *is* hot enough—and you fry it in a light oil—it will come out surprisingly light and delicate, like classic Japanese tempura.

Garlic Aïoli

The aïoli can be stored in a sealed glass container in the refrigerator for up to a week.

1 SMALL YUKON GOLD POTATO,
PEELED AND QUARTERED

4 GARLIC CLOVES, PEELED AND CHOPPED,
ABOUT 1 TABLESPOON

1 TABLESPOON DIJON MUSTARD

1 EGG YOLK

1/2 TEASPOON SEA SALT

1/4 TEASPOON FRESHLY GROUND BLACK PEPPER

1 CUP EXTRA-VIRGIN OLIVE OIL

JUICE OF 1/2 LEMON

1. Boil the potato in salted water until tender, about 20 minutes, then pass it through a food mill.

2. Add the potato, garlic, mustard, egg yolk, salt, and pepper to the bowl of a food processor and process until well mixed. Continue to process the mixture while adding the olive oil in a slow stream until it attains a mayonnaise-like consistency. Add the lemon juice, mix well, transfer to a serving bowl, and serve.

Tomato Sambal

This is the most basic tomato salad, given the Southeast Asian and Indian name for pickles or side dishes. It is simple to prepare, relies on the best fresh ingredients, and serves as a wonderful garnish or refresher alongside the stew and in addition to the chutney.

2 LARGE OR 3 MEDIUM RED TOMATOES,
SEEDED AND DICED

2 LARGE OR 3 MEDIUM YELLOW TOMATOES,
SEEDED AND DICED

2 TABLESPOONS COARSELY CHOPPED RED ONION

4 TABLESPOONS EXTRA-VIRGIN OLIVE OIL

2 TABLESPOONS RED WINE VINEGAR

COARSE SEA SALT AND FRESHLY GROUND BLACK
PEPPER, TO TASTE

1 TABLESPOON CHOPPED BASIL

Place the tomatoes and the chopped onion in a large serving bowl. Add the oil, vinegar, salt, pepper, and basil, toss well, and allow to rest at room temperature for up to 1 hour before serving.

TOMATO LAMB BREDIE

A bredie is the typical slow-cooked stew of Cape Malay cuisine, which is best when prepared in a heavy-bottom cast-iron pot or *potjie*. I've adapted it in a recipe that takes just over an hour to cook. Traditionally, this type of dish would probably have been made with just the lamb knuckles, but I've added the shoulder to provide some additional meat. The sweet and savory flavors are wholly authentic; the dish is like a curry with an extra measure of sweetness to balance the hot spice. You'll taste a delightful hint of cinnamon, which speaks unmistakably of the Orient. It's great with Aromatic Basmatic Rice.

4½ TABLESPOONS SUNFLOWER OIL
(OR SOME OTHER MEDIUM TO LIGHT VEGETABLE OIL)

2 LARGE YELLOW ONIONS, COARSELY CHOPPED
(ABOUT 4 CUPS)

3 BAY LEAVES

3 CINNAMON STICKS

2½ POUNDS LAMB KNUCKLES,
CUT INTO 1½-INCH CUBES

1½ POUNDS BONELESS LAMB SHOULDER,
CUT INTO 1½-INCH CUBES

3 TABLESPOONS ALL-PURPOSE FLOUR

¼ CUP WHITE WINE

1 LARGE RIPE TOMATO
(½ POUND), PEELED (SEE PAGE 57) AND CHOPPED

4 GARLIC CLOVES, CRUSHED

2 TEASPOONS COARSE SEA SALT

1 TEASPOON FRESHLY GROUND BLACK PEPPER

1 SPICY RED DRY CHILI PEPPER, CRUSHED
(APPROXIMATELY 1 TABLESPOON; THE AMOUNT CAN BE ADJUSTED
ACCORDING TO TASTE), OR ½ TABLESPOON HOT RED PEPPER FLAKES

2½ TABLESPOONS TOMATO PASTE

4 MEDIUM POTATOES, PEELED, QUARTERED,
AND PLACED IN A BOWL OF COLD WATER

2½ TABLESPOONS SUGAR

2 TABLESPOONS CHOPPED FLAT-LEAF PARSLEY
OR CILANTRO, FOR GARNISH

1 RECIPE AROMATIC BASMATI RICE (PAGE 119)

1. Place 2½ tablespoons of the oil in a large Dutch oven, Crock Pot, or cast-iron stew pot over medium heat. Add the onions, bay leaves, and cinnamon sticks and sauté, stirring constantly, for about 10 minutes, or until golden. Remove from the pot and set aside.

2. Dust the meat with flour and divide it into two batches. Add 1 tablespoon of oil to the pot over medium heat, add the first batch of meat, and brown on all sides, approximately 5 minutes. Remove the browned meat from the pot and set aside. Add the remaining tablespoon of oil to the pot and repeat the browning process for the second batch. Remove excess grease from the pot by using a large ladle or spoon.

3. Add the white wine to the pot, reduce the heat, and deglaze using a wooden spoon. Return the reserved meat and the onions, bay leaves, and cinnamon stick to the pot. Add the tomato, crushed garlic, salt and pepper, chili, and tomato paste. Cover the pot and simmer over medium heat for 40 minutes, stirring from time to time. Add the potatoes and sugar, and cook until tender, about 20 minutes. Remove the lid from the pot, stir, and cook, for a final 15 minutes. Garnish with chopped parsley or cilantro and serve the bredie hot with the rice on the side.

PEACH CHUTNEY

This recipe comes to us courtesy of Rani, author of *Feast of India: A Legacy of Recipes and Fables,* which is a really good basic Indian cookbook. Peach chutney has the sweetness and tanginess to create a beautiful counterbalance to the spices in the main dish.

½ CUP CIDER VINEGAR

15 GARLIC CLOVES, PEELED AND FINELY CHOPPED

1 1-INCH PIECE OF FRESH GINGERROOT,
PEELED AND FINELY CHOPPED

1 BAY LEAF

12 WHOLE PEPPERCORNS

½ TEASPOON GROUND MUSTARD SEED

1 CUP BROWN SUGAR

½ TEASPOON CAYENNE PEPPER

½ TEASPOON SALT

3 POUNDS FRESH RIPE PEACHES, PEELED (OPTIONAL),
PITTED, AND FINELY CHOPPED

1. Place a medium pot over medium heat. Add the vinegar, garlic, gingerroot, bay leaf, peppercorns, ground mustard seed, brown sugar, cayenne pepper, and salt, and stir constantly for 2 to 3 minutes. Add the peaches and mix thoroughly. Cover and simmer for 30 minutes, until the peaches are soft and mashed and the chutney is thick. Stir occasionally to prevent the ingredients from sticking to the bottom of the pot. Remove from the heat and allow to cool.

2. Serve the chutney in a small bowl. To store, transfer it to a 16-ounce airtight jar and refrigerate for up to a week.

CAPE BRANDY TART WITH BRANDY SAUCE

I can't remember a Christmas back at home when we didn't sit around the family table and enjoy my sister Anne's wonderful tart at the end of the meal. It's heartwarming and incredibly convenient: It can be made days in advance and frozen, with no effect on the delicious result. For Christmastime, add ½ cup glacéed cherries to the batter; these holiday treats are the red and green cherries, preserved in jars.

1 CUP PITTED, CHOPPED DATES

1 TEASPOON BAKING SODA

2 ½ TABLESPOONS UNSALTED BUTTER OR MARGARINE,
SOFTENED

1 CUP SUPERFINE SUGAR

1 LARGE EGG

1 ½ CUPS FLOUR

PINCH OF SALT

3 TEASPOONS BAKING POWDER

½ CUP PECANS OR WALNUTS, CHOPPED

BRANDY SAUCE (RECIPE FOLLOWS)

1 TO 2 CUPS WHIPPED CREAM, FOR TOPPING

1. Preheat the oven to 350°F.

2. Place the dates in a small bowl, pour 1 cup of boiling water over them, and add the baking soda. Let the dates stand for 10 minutes, or until soft.

3. In the bowl of an electric mixer with the beaters attached, combine the butter and sugar, and beat until creamy. Beat in the egg. Sift in the flour, salt, and baking powder. Add the date mixture, including the water, and the pecans. Mix well.

4. Line a lightly oiled or buttered 9-inch aluminum pie plate with parchment paper. (Alternatively, use a 9-inch springform pan.) Pour the date and nut mixture into the prepared plate and bake for 45 minutes, or until a toothpick inserted in the center comes out dry. To serve (see Note), remove from the pie plate, discard the parchment paper, allow to cool slightly, cut into wedges, and top with Brandy Sauce and whipped cream.

NOTE To store the tart, if made in advance: First, allow it to cool to room temperature. Then place it in a plastic freezer bag, expel the air, seal the bag, and place it in the freezer for up to one month. To reheat the tart, place it in a 250°F. oven until warm, about 45 minutes.

BRANDY SAUCE

½ CUP SUGAR
½ TABLESPOON UNSALTED BUTTER
½ TEASPOON VANILLA EXTRACT
¼ CUP BRANDY (OR RUM)

Combine the sugar with ¼ cup cold water in a saucepan over medium-high heat. Bring to a boil and continue to boil, stirring frequently, until the sugar is dissolved, about 5 minutes. Remove from the heat and stir in the butter and vanilla, followed by the brandy.

411: Whipped Cream

To make whipped cream, start with the freshest and finest heavy whipping cream you can find. The cream must be chilled for best results, so whip it straight out of the refrigerator. (Some chefs insist on chilling the bowl and utensil as well, but this is optional.) Cream can be whipped with an electric mixer, egg beaters, or a whisk, but the mixer has a tendency to over-whip it, so it's really best done by hand. It should be whipped just until it forms soft peaks— no more. Whipped cream can be stored in the refrigerator, in a covered glass or ceramic bowl, for a couple of hours, but it's best served fresh. If you like your whipped cream sweetened, add up to 2 tablespoons of granulated sugar per cup of cream during the whipping process. You can also add ½ teaspoon of vanilla powder for extra flavor.

Bombay Soirée
for 6

Our setting for this dinner was the Hamptons home of my friend the interior designer John Barman and his partner Kelly Graham, who expanded and renovated a modest ranch house near the beach into a stunning showcase. One of the keys to successful entertaining is staying flexible. We had planned to serve this meal at a long picnic table on John's ample flagstone patio, with drinks, picnic-style, on the lawn. We were expecting a balmy evening, but the weather didn't cooperate. The wind changed direction in the morning, the sky grew dark and stormy, and it rained periodically all day. So we happily moved our dinner indoors.

John's dining room has a round table worthy of King Arthur's Court, a cathedral-height ceiling, and huge windows that let in a tremendous amount of light, particularly helpful when the skies are brooding. The Indian hand-stitched tablecloth I had picked up on holiday in the Greek Isles a couple of weeks earlier was meant to be our picnic blanket, but it functioned very well as a covering for this magnificent table.

Beyond India's wonderfully flavorful foods, Indian design and decor have always been a great inspiration to me. I love the bright fabrics in vibrant shades of red and pink, elaborate patterns, and lacy gold-rimmed borders. Dressing up this dinner was a delightful experience.

For the centerpiece, I constructed a pyramid of spice. This might appear exceedingly complicated and expensive. But basically I used a worn old brass pedestal container and shaped a couple of cans of refried beans into a pyramid using the side of a dinner knife. I bought a one-pound bag of curry powder at an Indian market and used it to create large mounds. With a simple trompe-l'oeil trick like this, you can create an extravagant conversation piece. The appearance and the scent of this enormous mound of spice right in the middle of the table certainly takes your guests on a magical journey. You can be sure they'll be tickled when they see the lengths to which you've gone to transport them to faraway lands.

Of all the world cuisines I cook and serve, I think Indian is my favorite. I enjoyed early exposure to it where I grew up in southern Africa, which has one of the largest populations of Indians living outside India. In the Natal and Cape provinces of South Africa—especially in Cape Town and Durban, the cities along the Spice Route—Indian spices and recipes exert a major influence.

The beauty of this cuisine is the way it combines the remarkable variety of flavors and the degrees of hot, spicy, and sweet in its repertoire. A dish can include fifteen or twenty spices and other aromatic ingredients, but you never really taste any one; the coordination and harmony are miraculous. Indian food also possesses a major practical allure: The preparations are not complicated at all. Rather, it's about acquiring and combining a few key exotic ingredients with many other commonly available foods. With just a bit of planning and organization, you get a huge payout.

THE MENU: SUPPER FOR SIX

STIR-FRIED SHRIMP WITH LEMON AND SCALLIONS
YOGURT AND CUCUMBER RAITA
TOMATO AND ONION RAITA
YOGURT AND BANANA RAITA
MANGO CHUTNEY
CHICKEN CURRY WITH PEAS
AROMATIC BASMATI RICE
PAPPADUMS
SAMBALS

DESSERT
COCONUT MERINGUE WITH TROPICAL FRUIT
AND FRESH WHIPPED CREAM

TO DRINK
COCKTAIL DE NUIT: BEER SHANDY
WINE: RED AND WHITE WINE
FOR RED, I SELECTED A GOOD AUSTRALIAN SHIRAZ;
YOU CAN'T GO WRONG WITH THAT.
THE WHITE WAS A SOUTH AFRICAN SAUVIGNON BLANC.
THERE ARE ALSO TWO VERY GOOD INDIAN LAGER BEERS THAT
COMPLEMENT THE FOOD WELL: TAJ MAHAL AND KINGFISHER.

TIMING The shrimp can be marinated the morning of or well in advance of the guests' arrival; it takes literally a couple of minutes to cook. The curry takes about 1 hour and can be made a day in advance; in fact, this is one of those dishes that gets better with a little age. A day or two in the refrigerator gives its flavors time to meld and mature. The rice takes about 35 minutes. The raitas can also be made in advance, stored in the fridge, and placed on the table just before the meal.

BEER SHANDY

It's great to eat hot spicy foods in warm weather, and beer is an ideal drink to wash them down. The shandy is a traditional British summer drink consisting of half beer and half of what they call lemonade, which in America is sold under the brand names of 7-Up and Sprite. I like to drink a shandy well chilled; so just take both drinks right out of the fridge, combine them in glasses, and serve.

STIR-FRIED SHRIMP WITH LEMON AND SCALLIONS

Shrimp is a favorite in many cuisines and particularly in my kitchen. Its immense popularity and fabulous taste are matched by its ease of preparation. This dish involves two simple steps: marinating and quick frying. The best pan to use is a wok, which heats up quickly and gives strong, even heat distribution. This is my adaptation of a recipe from the accomplished Maya Kaimal and her book *Curried Favors.*

2 TEASPOONS GROUND CORIANDER

1 TEASPOON GROUND CUMIN

$1/2$ TEASPOON CAYENNE PEPPER

$1/2$ TEASPOON GROUND TURMERIC

2 TEASPOONS MINCED GARLIC

2 TEASPOONS MINCED PEELED FRESH GINGER

2 POUNDS LARGE SHRIMP
(U15 TO U20; SEE NOTE), SHELLED AND DEVEINED

4 TABLESPOONS PEANUT OIL
(OR, FOR AN INTERESTING FLAVOR TWIST, TOASTED SESAME OIL)

1 TEASPOON SALT

$1/2$ TEASPOON PEPPER

JUICE OF 1 LARGE LEMON (ABOUT 2 TABLESPOONS)

2 WHOLE SCALLIONS, WHITE AND GREEN PARTS,
THINLY SLICED ON THE BIAS

1. In a medium bowl, combine the coriander, cumin, cayenne, turmeric, garlic, and ginger. Place the shrimp in a glass dish, rub well with the spices, cover the dish with plastic wrap, and refrigerate for at least 1 hour.

2. Heat the peanut oil in a wok or large frying pan over high flame until it is nearly smoking. Add half the shrimp, along with half the salt and pepper, to the pan and cook, stirring continually, until the shrimp are almost opaque, about 2 minutes; do not overcook. Repeat the process for the second batch. (Cook the shrimp in two batches so they can remain in one layer in the pan.) Add the lemon juice and scallions, and continue cooking for an additional 30 seconds. Remove the pan from the heat, transfer the shrimp to bowls, and serve.

NOTE The size of shrimp is given by the number of them per pound; the larger the shrimp, the smaller the number per pound. Jumbo shrimp are generally under 15 per pound; large are 20 to 30 per pound; medium are up to 35 per pound; and small up to 45. Their sizes are often labeled as U30 (under 30 per pound), U20, U15, and so forth.

911 Firefighters

If you or any of your guests are shy when it comes to the flavor of hot, spicy peppers, some well-chilled cantaloupe, honeydew, or watermelon balls are a good antidote to put out the fire.

YOGURT AND CUCUMBER RAITA

MAKES ABOUT 2 CUPS

Any quality yogurt will do for this recipe (and for the Yogurt and Banana Raita opposite). But if you like rich, creamy yogurt, try using the Greek variety; it is the best for my money.

1/2 CUCUMBER, PEELED AND THINLY SLICED
1 CUP PLAIN YOGURT
2 TABLESPOONS CHOPPED CILANTRO
1/2 TEASPOON SALT
WHITE PEPPER, TO TASTE

Mix all the ingredients in a serving bowl, chill, and serve cool. The raita can be stored for up to 24 hours in the refrigerator, in a covered glass or ceramic container.

TOMATO AND ONION RAITA

MAKES ABOUT 3 CUPS

3 LARGE RIPE TOMATOES, SEEDED AND CUBED
1/2 MEDIUM WHITE ONION, FINELY CHOPPED
2 TABLESPOONS CHOPPED CILANTRO
1/2 GREEN CHILI, SEEDED AND CHOPPED
1/3 CUP RED WINE VINEGAR
(OR BROWN ENGLISH CIDER VINEGAR)
2 TABLESPOONS OLIVE OIL
1 TABLESPOON SUGAR
SALT AND FRESHLY GROUND BLACK PEPPER, TO TASTE

1. Place the tomatoes, onion, cilantro, and chili in a bowl, and mix well.
2. Prepare the vinaigrette: In a medium bowl, whisk together the vinegar, oil, sugar, and salt and pepper to taste. Pour the vinaigrette over the tomato mixture along with 2 tablespoons of water, refrigerate for up to 2 hours, and serve. This raita can be stored in a covered glass or ceramic container in the refrigerator for up to 24 hours.

SAMBALS

Curries are usually served with fruit and vegetable chutneys as well as sambals, those charming, ubiquitous, and often pickled little side dishes or condiments that are prevalent throughout Malaysia, Indonesia, and southern India. This is one of the aspects I love most about the cuisine: Amid spicy, sweet, and pungent aromas wafting through the air, the table is dotted with plates of delicious tidbits of complementary and contrasting flavors—ideal for sampling here and there, mixing and matching. All of this makes for a lively and stimulating backdrop to the social interaction of a dinner party.

In a traditional Indian feast, the main course is served with the sambals on the side. They should be served chilled, because they provide contrast to the heat—temperature-wise and spice-wise—of the principal dishes. Whether I had a round or a square table for this meal, I'd place a large wooden serving tray of the same shape in the center; as the finishing touch to setting the table, I'd surround the tray with bowls of the sambals so they could be sampled at any time during the meal. In addition to the raitas, I suggest serving several fruit chutneys and possibly some achars or pickles, which can be purchased at Indian markets, gourmet delis, and most well-stocked supermarkets.

Yogurt and Banana Raita

MAKES ABOUT 3 CUPS

2 LARGE BANANAS, PEELED AND SLICED
1 CUP PLAIN YOGURT
2 TABLESPOONS DARK RAISINS
1 TABLESPOON CHOPPED CILANTRO (OPTIONAL)

Mix all the ingredients in a serving bowl, chill, and serve cool.

Mango Chutney

Rani has written a remarkable cookbook entitled *Feast of India,* in which she demystifies Indian cuisine, providing many straightforward, easy-to-prepare, and extremely tasty recipes. She was kind enough to lend us her recipes for Mango Chutney and Garam Masala (page 119) for this chapter and for Peach Chutney (for "Africa, My Home," page 108).

MAKES ABOUT 2 CUPS

6 FIRM, HALF-RIPE MANGOES, PEELED AND SLICED THIN
1 CUP CIDER VINEGAR
1 CUP PACKED LIGHT BROWN SUGAR
10 GARLIC CLOVES, PEELED AND SLICED
1 1-INCH PIECE OF FRESH GINGER,
PEELED AND SLICED THIN
1 TEASPOON GROUND DRIED RED CHILIES
OR CAYENNE PEPPER
SALT, TO TASTE

Place all the ingredients in a medium pot over medium-high heat. Bring to a boil, reduce the heat to low, and simmer for 30 to 40 minutes, stirring occasionally to prevent sticking. Remove the pan from the heat and allow the chutney to cool before serving. To store, transfer to an airtight jar and refrigerate for up to a week.

411: Choosing Mangoes

Mangoes start out green and turn yellow with lovely reddish highlights as they ripen. A ripe mango should be somewhat soft or pliant. As with many fruits, slightly unripe ones can be sealed in a paper bag for a day or two to ripen. Green mangoes are used for pickling and meat tenderizing in India and Southeast Asia. Most recipes for mango chutney call for mangoes that are half-ripe or quite firm.

411: Key Indian Ingredients and Food Terms

Achar (or *Atchar*) A pickled and/or salted relish; they range from sweet to hot.

Basmati Rice: A fine, long-grained variety of rice that has been grown in the foothills of the Himalayas since ancient times. Basmati is aged after harvesting to give it its characteristic nutty flavor and perfumed aroma.

Curry: Kari is an all-purpose Indian culinary term that means "sauce." Curries come in powdered form and also as oils or pastes, and are the basis for curry dishes, which can be meat, vegetable, or fish. Curry powder is a blend of toasted spices that commonly includes cardomom, cinnamon, cloves, coriander, cumin, fennel seed, fenugreek, mace, nutmeg, black pepper, and dried hot chili peppers. Curry powders can retain their flavors for up to six months if carefully stored in airtight containers. Curry pastes, made from the powder combined with vegetable oil and/or vinegar, can last up to one month if stored in an airtight container in the refrigerator.

Curry Leaves: Similar to bay leaves or small shiny lemon leaves, the leaves of this herb have a distinct curry flavor. Available fresh in most Indian markets.

Garam Masala: The *masala,* or "mix," is the basic ingredient of a curry; *garam masala* means "hot spice." Indian chefs are like master alchemists when it comes to combining herbs and spices; they use as many as twenty to create a garam masala. Each recipe is highly personalized and relies on centuries of cooking science and lore.

Raita: Refreshing yogurt salads designed to balance the hot, spicy aspect of much of the cuisine. In addition to yogurt, they include chopped fruits or vegetables and herbs or spices. The quintessential raita is yogurt-cucumber.

Chicken Curry and Peas

I filmed one of my television shows in South Africa with Pat Maistrey, the chef at the Zimbali Lodge. He took me on a tour of the spice market in Durban, where we selected our ingredients, and we returned to his kitchen totally inspired and prepared this dish together. I make many different curries, and this is one of my favorites. It's easy, fun, and trouble-free—not to mention utterly delicious. This is a medium-spicy curry; you can increase or decrease the heat by adjusting the quantity of chili powder according to taste.

1/3 cup olive oil

2 medium yellow onions, finely chopped

3 garlic cloves, crushed

4 tablespoons chopped peeled fresh ginger

1 1/2 tablespoons ground cumin

1 1/2 tablespoons Garam Masala (recipe follows)

1 1/2 tablespoons ground coriander

3/4 tablespoon chili powder or cayenne pepper
(or less if you prefer a milder curry)

1 tablespoon ground turmeric

3 large tomatoes, cubed

2/3 cup tomato paste

1 chicken (2 1/2 to 3 pounds),
skin removed, back removed, and cut into 8 pieces

2 chicken breasts,
skin removed, bone in, halved crosswise

1/2 teaspoon coarse sea salt, plus more to taste

1 1/2 cups peas
(fresh or frozen; if fresh, parboil for 5 minutes in advance)

20 whole fresh curry leaves (if available)

2 tablespoons coarsely chopped fresh cilantro

1. Place the oil in a large cast-iron pot over medium heat. Add the onions, garlic, and ginger and sauté for about 5 minutes, or until the onion is transparent. Stir in the cumin, garam masala, coriander, chili powder, and turmeric, and sauté for another 2 minutes.
2. Add the tomatoes and tomato paste. Cover the pan and sauté for another 2 minutes, then add 1 cup of water (see Note). Add the chicken, cover the pan again, reduce the heat to medium-low, and simmer for 25 minutes. Season to taste with salt.
3. Add the peas, curry leaves, and cilantro. Cover the pot and simmer for 10 minutes, until the sauce is thick and the peas are cooked. Serve with rice.

NOTE If the sauce needs thickening, dissolve a couple of tablespoons of cornstarch in about 1/4 cup warm water, then stir some of the mixture into the curry. Continue to stir in small amounts of the dissolved cornstarch until the sauce reaches your desired thickness, being careful to allow each successive addition to react with the liquid before adding more; you don't want to end up with an overly thick and glue-like sauce.

If you'd like to add even more substance to this stew, add two or three medium potatoes, cut into small cubes, when you add the peas.

GARAM MASALA

You can buy this in a store, or for an extra touch of authenticity make it yourself. Thanks again to Rani for lending us her recipe from *Feast of India*.

I CUP BLACK OR BROWN CARDAMOM,
PODS REMOVED AND DISCARDED, LEAVING THE SEEDS
5 CINNAMON STICKS, BROKEN INTO SMALL PIECES
1/4 CUP BLACK PEPPERCORNS
1/4 CUP CARAWAY OR CUMIN SEEDS
2 TABLESPOONS WHOLE CLOVES
1/4 WHOLE NUTMEG, GRATED

Place the cardamon, cinnamon, peppercorns, cumin, cloves, and nutmeg in a small, heavy-bottomed frying pan or on an iron griddle over medium heat. Roast them, stirring constantly, until the spices turn a shade darker, 4 to 5 minutes; do not let them burn. Remove the pan from the heat and transfer the spices to a spice or coffee grinder. Grind to a fine powder. Store in an airtight jar.

AROMATIC BASMATI RICE

As always, the simplest way to prepare rice is in a rice cooker (see page 95), but the recipe below is made without one.

I TABLESPOON UNSALTED BUTTER
I GARLIC CLOVE, CRUSHED
1/2 RED BELL PEPPER,
SEEDS REMOVED AND CUT INTO 1/4-INCH CUBES
1/2 YELLOW BELL PEPPER,
SEEDS REMOVED AND CUT INTO 1/4-INCH CUBES
1/2 CUP CHOPPED YELLOW ONION
(FROM I MEDIUM ONION)
1/2 TEASPOON GROUND TURMERIC
I 1/2 CUPS WHITE BASMATI RICE, WELL RINSED
3 CUPS CHICKEN STOCK (RECIPE FOLLOWS) OR WATER
1/4 CUP GOLDEN RAISINS
1/4 CUP DARK RAISINS
I CINNAMON STICK
1/2 TEASPOON SALT
3 TABLESPOONS SLIVERED ALMONDS, TOASTED
(SEE NOTE)
6 WHOLE SPRIGS OF CILANTRO, FOR GARNISH

1. Melt the butter in a large skillet over medium heat. Reduce the heat to low and add the garlic, bell peppers, onion, and turmeric. Cook uncovered for 10 minutes, or until the onion becomes translucent.

2. Add the rice, stock or water, raisins, cinnamon, and salt. Bring to a boil, then reduce the heat to low; cover and cook for 20 minutes, or until the liquid is absorbed by the rice.

3. Remove the pan from the heat and keep it covered for 5 minutes. Fluff the rice with a fork and discard the cinnamon. Transfer the rice to a serving platter, top it with the toasted almonds and cilantro sprigs, and serve.

NOTE Toast the almond slivers by placing them in a skillet over medium heat until they turn a shade darker, about 3 minutes; alternatively, place them on a baking sheet in a 300°F. oven for 3 to 5 minutes. Be careful not to burn them. Remove the nuts immediately from the pan and pour them into a glass or ceramic vessel to prevent further toasting.

CHICKEN STOCK

The stock can be refrigerated in a covered container for 3 or 4 days; it can also be frozen for up to a month.

I 4-POUND STEWING CHICKEN OR ROASTER
(OR THE EQUIVALENT IN CHICKEN PARTS AND CARCASSES)
I LARGE YELLOW ONION, ROUGHLY CHOPPED
2 OR 3 RIBS CELERY, ROUGHLY CHOPPED
2 OR 3 MEDIUM CARROTS, ROUGHLY CHOPPED
I BOUQUET GARNI (SEE NOTE)
I TEASPOON SALT, PLUS MORE TO TASTE
I HEAD GARLIC, CUT IN HALF HORIZONTALLY

1. Combine all the ingredients in a large stockpot and add 4 quarts of water. Bring the pot to a boil, lower the heat so the broth is just simmering, partially cover the pot, and cook for 1 to 2 hours.
2. Strain the contents of the pot, pressing on the solids to extract all the juices. Allow the stock to cool, then refrigerate. Before using, skim the hardened fat off the top of the stock.

NOTE A classic bouquet garni features thyme, parsley, and bay leaf either tied with string or wrapped in a small packet of cheese-cloth; I also add some leek green. You could include oregano, marjoram, or basil if you like. To make a bouquet garni, cut the green part off a leek and gather it into a bunch with 1 sprig of thyme, 1 bay leaf, and 1 sprig of parsley. Tie them all together and use the bouquet to season soups and stews.

PAPPADAMS

Pappadams (also spelled *poppadum* or *pappadom*) are wafer-thin crispy savory breads made from lentil flour and various spices—the Indian equivalent to a Mexican tortilla. They provide the ideal accompaniment to the hearty curry and its refreshing side dishes. You can purchase pappadams prepared but uncooked at Indian markets, gourmet delis, and many super-markets; cook according to the instructions on the package. This usually means deep-frying in hot oil for 2 seconds on each side, then draining on paper towels. (Be sure a pappadam is fully submerged in ½ to ¾ inch of oil for frying.) Pappadams can be cooked in advance, but they must be stored in an airtight container, as humidity will render them soggy. You can serve them before the meal with drinks or during the appetizer course.

Coconut Meringue with Tropical Fruit and Fresh Whipped Cream

The meringues bake for 2 to 3 hours in the oven on low heat, so it's advisable to make them a day or two in advance and store them in an airtight container. Bake them Sunday for a Tuesday-night dinner, or simply buy them prepared in a store.

When choosing passion fruit, remember that the more wrinkled the skin, the sweeter the pulp will be.

4 LARGE EGG WHITES (OR 1/2 CUP)
PINCH OF SALT
1/2 CUP GRANULATED SUGAR
3/4 CUP CONFECTIONERS' SUGAR
2 OUNCES UNSWEETENED SHREDDED COCONUT
2 KIWI, PEELED AND CUBED
1 MANGO, PEELED AND CUBED
1 PAPAYA, PEELED AND CUBED
1 PINT MANGO SORBET
1 BATCH OF FRESH WHIPPED CREAM (SEE PAGE 109)
6 FRESH PASSION FRUITS, HALVED

1. Preheat the oven to 200°F.
2. Cover a baking sheet with parchment paper and draw twelve 2½-inch circles on the paper with a pencil.
3. Whip the egg whites, along with the pinch of salt, in an electric mixer on high speed. Gradually add the granulated sugar until the mixture is thick and glossy.
4. Gently fold the confectioners' sugar and coconut into the egg white mixture with a spatula. Stir until well combined.
5. Using a large spoon, place an equal amount of the mixture within each circle on the parchment paper. Build "nests" by creating indentations in the middle of each mound. Bake the nests for 2 to 3 hours, until the meringues are dry and can be removed from the paper without sticking to your finger.
6. To assemble the dessert, place one meringue in the center of each of 6 plates, distribute equal portions of the kiwi, mango, and papaya around each meringue, place a scoop of sorbet in each nest, and top with another meringue to form a sandwich. Top the sandwich with whipped cream and drizzle the pulp and juice of one passion fruit over each.

OTT
Use a piping bag to squeeze the meringue batter onto the baking sheet and form a swirling pattern.

A CASE-STUDY DINNER
FOR 6

I was California dreaming on a winter's day—or maybe it was late spring. Anyhow, I was thinking fondly, nostalgically about the friends I left in Los Angeles when I moved to the East Coast. I lived in L.A. for thirteen years, and my connections to the people and the place are still strong. I decided the next time I was in town and had a free evening, I'd organize a small reunion.

When I first moved to Los Angeles, I toured many houses from the outside. This gem, in the hills of Bel Air, was always among my favorites. Ironically, I had long since moved to New York before I had ever set foot in it. Through a series of fortunate coincidences, my friend Reagan Silver became its owner, and my best friend, the extraordinary interior designer Charles Allem, renovated its interior. It is an absolutely stunning piece of architecture, perched on a ledge with expansive views spreading toward the horizon. At night, the house seems to float above the shimmering lights of the city below.

The house is poured concrete and reinforced steel construction, with a large open plan and floor-to-ceiling glass on the "view" side. Very much in the avant-garde, a real case-study house, it was designed by Richard Dorman in the Post and Beam Style, which is rare for this type of architecture, and built in 1964. Charles brought back its original glory, opening up the interior spaces and creating room to breathe. He introduced numerous shades of green as the accent color, right down to the collection of chartreuse martini and champagne glasses lining the shelves of the well-stocked bar.

The guests were my close friends Karyn and Joel Silver (no relation to Reagan), along with photographer Lyndie Benson, Judy Feder, and my partner Stuart Brownstein. Joel's latest action-packed film had opened to a superb box office, so if the reunion wasn't enough of an excuse to celebrate, then the opening-weekend success certainly was.

What could be better than bringing old friends together in such a spectacular setting? Karyn, Joel, Judy, Lyndie, and I all share a love of great architecture, so it was doubly exhilarating to stage our reunion in this sensational structure. Given the clean, spare lines of the house, reflected in a well-edited interior design and decor, I wanted my table setting and party plan to fall in line. In this ambience, less is definitely more. For the table, I found a wonderful pod plant called a Star of Bethlehem, which in its green stage has almost no flowers. I assembled the stars in long stainless-steel

Music

You can make your own CDs now with a piece of hardware called a CD burner that allows you to create compilations. The new CD from your favorite artist will have three songs you love and nine you hate. Now, you can make your own selections for various scenarios and occasions: dinners, parties, car trips, and so forth. Whenever I buy a new CD, I review it and select the tracks I like, divide them into categories—cocktail music, dinner music, after-dinner music, opera, and so forth—for when I'm ready to make compilations. You can easily put five hours of music on one CD, which will cover an entire evening (including preparation time). There are no breaks for changing CDs; things run smoothly from start to finish, right down to the music. You can also make copies of your compilations; they make great gifts for many occasions.

If you're not inclined to make your own compilations, there are other good sources. I love the CDs created by Claude Challe, the DJ originally from the Buddha Bar in Paris. He has a great gift when it comes to mixing and pairing music. In general, if you have got a favorite club or bar or hangout (even your gym or health club) where you really enjoy the music, try to obtain copies of their CDs. Most places make their own these days, and they're usually willing to give them away to preferred customers.

troughs down the center of the table; then I studded the table with square black and brown candles.

I wanted this to be a leisurely yet sexy feast with remarkable flavors that matched the spirit of the occasion. The food should be sophisticated and spicy, yet uncomplicated and manageable. The meal took on a modern, updated Southern African–Indian theme. With the exception of the lamb chops, which are started in the pan and then finished briefly in the oven, the entire meal, including dessert, is conveniently prepared on the stovetop.

Only the Best

I can't emphasize enough the importance of searching out the best ingredients. They are the basis for your meal; they determine the eventual success of your recipes. Wherever you live, take the time to discover where you can get the finest produce as well as top-quality store-bought or prepared foods. There's nothing wrong with including prepared foods in your menu. Get rid of your guilt, forget the notion that a meal is somehow inauthentic because you didn't make *every single item* from scratch. When you serve a cocktail, after all, you don't make the vodka. Besides, a savvy host today is a resourceful one. Remember: You get no medals for chopping, slicing, dicing, and making it all from scratch—especially when it's available premade.

The Menu: Supper for Six

Appetizers
Watermelon, Tomato, and Basil Salad
Corn-and-Crab Fritters with Lemon Mayonnaise

Main Courses
Pan-Roasted Spiced Lamb Chops
with Mango Chutney
Red Lentils
Curried Cauliflower

Dessert
Caramelized Bananas with Rum-Raisin Ice Cream

To Drink
Cocktail de Nuit: Vodka Tonic with Mint
Wine: Côtes du Rhône
from Guigal or some comparably good producer; this fine
Southern Rhône red has the balance, body, and spicy
accents to pair beautifully with the lamb chops.

Vodka Tonic with Mint

Sometimes all it takes to jazz up an old standby and make it really exciting is a simple twist. In this case the "twist" is a small handful of mint leaves.

12 ounces top-quality vodka
25 ounces tonic water
25 to 30 fresh mint leaves

For each drink, fill a highball glass with ice, pour in 2 ounces of vodka, fill the remainder of the glass with tonic water, add 4 or 5 mint leaves, stir well, and serve.

TIMING The salad can be prepared quickly just before serving or made in advance and refrigerated if you like. The batter or dough for the fritters needs to sit for 30 minutes before frying; the fritters can be cooked in advance of the guests' arrival, then reheated, or they can be fried at the end of the cocktail hour, drained, and served immediately. Likewise, the lamb chops need to marinate for a half hour; they can be prepped in advance. The lamb chops can be seared before the guests arrive, then finished in the oven just prior to serving. The lentils take about 30 to 35 minutes total for preparation and cooking; they can be made in advance and kept warm in the oven. Ditto the cauliflower.

WATERMELON, TOMATO, AND BASIL SALAD

Simplicity and Style

At cocktail parties, I often serve toasted cheese sandwiches. People will exclaim, "Oh my goodness, this is so delicious!" And it will be if you keep it simple, get the best ingredients, do it right, and present it in style. It's one of the most basic foods and it's utterly delicious: Two slices of bread, some butter, a sprinkling of cayenne pepper, and some genuine imported Cheddar toasted in a pan. Serve it with an elegant glass of white wine, chilled in an ice bucket, and you've got an instant cocktail party.

This light, refreshing, and exceedingly tasty salad was inspired by my friend Geoffrey Zakarian, chef and owner at the fabulous Manhattan restaurant Town.

¹/₂ RED AND/OR YELLOW SEEDLESS WATERMELON
(ABOUT 4 POUNDS), CUT INTO 1-INCH CUBES

30 RED AND/OR YELLOW CHERRY TOMATOES, HALVED

10 SMALL BASIL LEAVES
FROM THE CENTER OF THE SPRIG

¹/₄ CUP BALSAMIC VINEGAR

¹/₂ CUP OLIVE OIL

COARSE SEA SALT AND FRESHLY
GROUND BLACK PEPPER, TO TASTE

1. Combine the watermelon, tomatoes, and basil in a large serving bowl.
2. Place the vinegar in a small mixing bowl, whisk in the oil, add the mixture to the salad, and toss well. Season with salt and pepper, and serve either chilled or at room temperature.

CORN-AND-CRAB FRITTERS WITH LEMON MAYONNAISE

Fritters were always a big part of the cuisine in my native southern Africa. As a kid, I remember we had all kinds—pumpkin fritters, banana fritters with brown sugar for dessert, and of course these corn-and-crab delights. They are unbelievably delicious, and can be prepared in advance and warmed up just before serving. The lemon mayonnaise, which can also be prepared in advance, provides just the right element of flavor and texture contrast; for a different accompaniment, try the Garlic Aïoli.

2 EARS YELLOW SWEET CORN
(OR 1 CUP FROZEN KERNELS, THAWED)

1 TABLESPOON UNSALTED BUTTER

1 MEDIUM YELLOW ONION, FINELY CHOPPED
(ABOUT ½ CUP)

1 CUP FLOUR, SIFTED

1 TEASPOON BAKING POWDER

⅔ CUP WHOLE MILK

1 POUND FRESH LUMP JUMBO CRABMEAT,
PICKED OVER TO MAKE SURE NO FRAGMENTS OF SHELL REMAIN

2 LARGE EGGS

⅛ TEASPOON CAYENNE PEPPER

1 TEASPOON COARSE SEA SALT

½ TEASPOON FRESHLY GROUND BLACK PEPPER

VEGETABLE OIL FOR PAN-FRYING (ABOUT 1 CUP)

LEMON MAYONNAISE (RECIPE FOLLOWS)
OR GARLIC AÏOLI (PAGE 106)

1. Cut the kernels off the ears of corn using a sharp kitchen knife.
2. Place the butter in a medium saucepan over medium-low heat. Add the onion and corn and cook, stirring occasionally, for 10 to 15 minutes, until the onion is soft. Remove from the heat and set aside to cool.
3. To prepare the dough, combine the flour and baking powder in a large mixing bowl. Add the milk slowly while stirring with a whisk; mix until smooth. Add the corn-onion mixture and the crab, and mix well. Add the eggs, cayenne pepper, salt, and black pepper, and continue mixing until all the ingredients are well incorporated. Cover the bowl with plastic wrap and refrigerate for 30 minutes, allowing the dough to set.
4. In a deep pan or cast-iron pot over medium flame, heat ¼ inch of oil until it just begins to smoke. While the oil is heating up, scoop up a tablespoon at a time of the dough and form flat patties. (They may be somewhat amorphous, but they will firm up when fried.) Using a large slotted spoon or spatula, slide the patties into the oil, one at a time. Fry until golden brown, about 1 minute per side. Drain the fritters on paper towels, and serve with lemon mayonnaise or garlic aïoli.

NOTE If you're frying the fritters in advance, set them aside after draining, then reheat them in the microwave on high for 25 to 40 seconds or in a 350°F. oven for 5 to 10 minutes.

LEMON MAYONNAISE

1 LARGE EGG YOLK

1 TEASPOON DIJON MUSTARD

½ TEASPOON SALT, PLUS MORE TO TASTE

¼ TEASPOON FRESHLY GROUND BLACK PEPPER,
PLUS MORE TO TASTE

1 CUP OLIVE OIL

JUICE OF ½ LEMON

ZEST OF ½ LEMON, FINELY CHOPPED

In a large mixing bowl (see Note), combine the egg yolk, mustard, and salt and pepper, and mix well. Stir the mixture briskly with a whisk while slowly adding the olive oil until it reaches the consistency of mayonnaise. Add the lemon juice and zest, and mix well. Adjust the seasonings and serve.

NOTE The mayonnaise can also be prepared in the bowl of a food processor with the metal blade attached: Simply combine all the ingredients except the oil and pulse until well mixed; then run the processor for 30 seconds to 1 minute while slowly adding the oil. The mayonnaise can be stored in a sealed glass jar in the refrigerator for up to a week.

Pan-Roasted Spiced Lamb Chops with Mango Chutney

The main course is one of my favorite dishes, which I discovered quite by chance when I was looking for a way to spice up lamp chops. It contains the same spice combination as Tandoori marinade but excludes the yogurt. I like to serve these chops with a good mango chutney, making for a classic contrast between the sweet chutney and the pungent spices.

1 TABLESPOON CURRY POWDER

2 TABLESPOONS GROUND CORIANDER

2 TABLESPOONS GROUND CUMIN

2 TABLESPOONS HOT PAPRIKA

2 TABLESPOONS GROUND GINGER

1 TABLESPOON GROUND TURMERIC

1 TABLESPOON CHILI POWDER

1/2 TABLESPOON GROUND CARDAMOM

1/2 TABLESPOON GROUND CINNAMON

18 RIB LAMB CHOPS, 1 1/2 TO 2 INCHES THICK
(SINGLE OR DOUBLE-BONED)

3 TABLESPOONS VEGETABLE OIL

2 TABLESPOONS COARSE SEA SALT

1 TABLESPOON FRESHLY GROUND BLACK PEPPER

1 RECIPE MANGO CHUTNEY (PAGE 117)

1. Preheat the oven to 400°F.

2. In a large, shallow bowl, combine the curry powder, coriander, cumin, paprika, ginger, turmeric, chili, cardamom, and cinnamon. Mix well. Press each chop into the powder to create a thick coating on each side. Place in a ceramic bowl or glass dish, cover, and marinate at room temperature for 1/2 hour.

3. Place 1 tablespoon of the vegetable oil in a large cast-iron skillet over medium heat. Season the lamb chops with the salt and pepper. When the oil is hot but not smoking, place 6 of the chops in the pan and cook until deep, dark brown (or "blackened" as in the famous New Orleans blackened redfish), about 2 minutes on each side. Remove the cooked chops, add another tablespoon of oil, and repeat for the remaining two batches. As each batch is complete, place the chops on a baking sheet.

4. Once all the chops are blackened, place the baking sheet in the oven for 5 to 6 minutes. For medium rare, the meat should be springy to the touch. Serve with mango chutney.

NOTE The chops can also be cooked entirely in the broiler.

RED LENTILS

Lentils are a staple food of India. Along with beans and peas, they are known as *dal,* or dried legumes. Dal dishes are inexpensive, highly nutritious, and very tasty. These lentils are one of the more delicate, subtle forms of dal, and they provide an excellent accompaniment to our lamb dish.

2 1/2 CUPS SMALL RED LENTILS
I TABLESPOON UNSALTED BUTTER
I CUP FINELY DICED ONION (FROM I MEDIUM ONION)
I TABLESPOON MINCED GARLIC
I TABLESPOON MINCED GINGER
I TEASPOON TURMERIC POWDER
I TEASPOON CORIANDER POWDER
1/2 TEASPOON CHILI POWDER
2 BAY LEAVES
4 CURRY LEAVES
I TABLESPOON COARSE SEA SALT
I TABLESPOON BROWN SUGAR
4 TABLESPOONS STORE-BOUGHT TAMARIND CHUTNEY
I TABLESPOON CHOPPED CILANTRO

1. Place the lentils in a colander and wash thoroughly with cold running water.
2. Place the butter in a heavy-bottomed pot over medium heat. Add the onion and sauté until soft, about 15 minutes. Add the garlic, ginger, turmeric, coriander, chili, bay leaves, curry leaves, lentils, salt, and enough water to cover by 1 inch. Bring to a boil over high heat, reduce the heat to low, partially cover the pot, and simmer for 30 to 40 minutes; add more water as necessary if the pot starts to dry up. When the lentils are done, remove the pot from the heat, stir in the brown sugar, tamarind chutney, and chopped cilantro, and serve.

CURRIED CAULIFLOWER

Cauliflower is extremely healthful, but it tends to be a bit bland. The fresh ginger and curry powder give it a delightful aromatic flavor, and they also turn it a lovely golden brown color.

2 LARGE HEADS OF CAULIFLOWER
1/4 CUP VEGETABLE OIL
I LARGE WHITE ONION, DICED
2 TABLESPOONS PEELED AND FINELY
CHOPPED FRESH GINGER
2 TABLESPOONS CURRY POWDER
I LARGE TOMATO, DICED
COARSE SEA SALT AND FRESHLY
GROUND BLACK PEPPER, TO TASTE

1. Bring a large pot of salted water to a boil, add the cauliflower, and cook over high heat for 10 minutes, or until al dente. Drain the cauliflower in a colander, refresh with cold running water, then separate the heads into small florets; discard the stems.
2. Place the oil in a large frying pan over medium heat. When the oil is hot, add the onion and ginger and cook for about 5 minutes, or until browned. Add the curry powder, stir, and continue to cook for 1 minute, or until the spice is evenly distributed. Add the tomato and continue cooking for 5 minutes, or until it is soft. Add the cauliflower florets, reduce the heat to medium-low, and continue cooking for an additional 5 minutes, stirring continuously. Season with salt and pepper and serve.

Caramelized Bananas with
Rum-Raisin Ice Cream

Talk about a dramatic finale: There isn't any cooking technique that matches flambéing. It takes a little patience and nerve, but the lasting impression is well worth the trouble.

1 CUP SUGAR

6 BANANAS, PEELED AND CUT INTO THIRDS ON THE BIAS

APPROXIMATELY 1/2 CUP DARK RUM

1 PINT RUM-RAISIN ICE CREAM

1. Melt the sugar in a large frying pan over medium heat until it starts to caramelize. Add the bananas, stir constantly with a wooden spoon, and cook for approximately 2 minutes, until they are evenly coated with the caramel mixture. Do not overcook the bananas; they should remain firm.

2. To flambé, hold your thumb over the open neck of the bottle of rum and sprinkle approximately 1/2 cup of the rum into the pan. The fumes from the rum will ignite once the liquid itself becomes hot enough. Continue to stir with the wooden spoon, angling the spoon in from the side and being careful not to come in contact with the flame. Tilt the pan (away from you) if necessary to encourage the flame. When the flame subsides, transfer the bananas and their sauce to individual bowls and serve with ice cream on the side.

The Menu: Supper for Six

Appetizers
Spice-Dusted Toasted Peanuts
Tortilla Soup

Main Course
Red Snapper à la Veracruzana
Cilantro Rice

Dessert
Ginger Flan

To Drink
Cocktail de Nuit: Mangorita or Sangrita
Wine: Spanish Red
A Tempranillo-based Spanish wine, such as Tinto Pesquera
from Ribera del Duero, has the fruit, the earthiness,
and the exotic hints to pair beautifully with the Mexican
spices but not to overpower the red snapper.

TIMING The soup can be made in advance and reheated. The fish sauce can be prepared in advance as well; the fillets themselves take about 5 minutes to cook. The flan for dessert requires about 30 minutes of prep time, followed by about 45 minutes of baking and 1 to 2 hours of refrigeration, so it's best made the night before or the morning of.

Cocktails de Nuit

I don't normally practice sex discrimination at cocktail hour, but in this case, with a nod to good old-fashioned south-of-the-border machismo, I decided to offer separate ladies' and men's libations. (Of course, people from either sex could feel free to choose either drink.) For the ladies, I made Mangoritas, a variation on a Margarita that features mango pulp. For the men, I served a drink called a Sangrita. (*Sangre* is Spanish for "blood" and *-ita* is the diminutive suffix; so this would translate literally as "little blood" or "bloodlet.") The Sangrita comprises two shots back to back, the first of tequila and the second of a mixture of chilies, onion, orange and tomato juices, lime, and salt, which adds up to something like a Mexican Bloody Mary. Strictly hardcore!

Mangorita

This, of course, is a variation on the classic Margarita with mango pulp instead of the usual lime juice. You can prepare it shaken over ice, or make a frozen version in the blender.

12 ounces tequila

4 ounces Triple Sec

1 cup peeled, sliced fresh mango
(from 1 large or 2 medium mangoes;
or substitute 1/2 pint mango sorbet)

1. Chill 6 martini glasses (see page 181).
2. Place all the ingredients in a blender full of ice and blend until smooth. Pour into chilled martini glasses and serve.

Sangrita

1 tablespoon minced fresh green
hot chili pepper (such as jalapeño or serrano;
adjust amount according to taste)

9 ounces orange juice

3 ounces tomato juice

2 tablespoons fresh lime juice
(from 1 medium lime)

2 tablespoons finely chopped white onion

1 teaspoon salt

12 ounces high-quality aged tequila

Place the minced pepper, orange juice, tomato juice, lime juice, onion, and salt in a blender and pulse until smooth. Strain the liquid into shot glasses. Serve alongside 1½- to 2-ounce shots of tequila.

Spice-Dusted Toasted Peanuts

If you're serving a potent drink or two, it's always a welcome touch—not to mention prudent and polite—to provide cocktail munchies. Instead of the standard chips, dips, and salsas, why not try something a little more intriguing, such as these tasty toasted nuts? And for an added color accent, you might garnish them with some beautiful little dried red chili peppers.

1 teaspoon ground coriander

1 teaspoon ground cumin

1/2 teaspoon cayenne pepper

1 tablespoon olive oil

1 pound raw peanuts, shelled

2 teaspoons salt, or to taste

1/4 teaspoon freshly ground black pepper

10 to 12 whole dried small red chili peppers,
for garnish (optional)

1. In a small mixing bowl, combine the coriander, cumin, and cayenne. Set aside.
2. Place the olive oil in a sauté pan over medium-high heat, add the peanuts, and toast them, stirring continually, until they are lightly browned, 4 to 5 minutes.
3. Dust the peanuts with the spices and toast for another 2 to 3 minutes. Season with the salt and pepper and then spread out to cool on a bed of paper towel. Once cool, place in a bowl and serve with the whole chili peppers as garnish.

Tortilla Soup

This is one of my all-time favorite soups, and I've encountered many variations of it through the years. The best one, in my opinion, comes from the Hotel Bel-Air in Los Angeles, and is the inspiration for our streamlined version here.

VEGETABLE OIL FOR DEEP-FRYING

8 6-INCH FLOUR TORTILLAS, JULIENNED
(CUT INTO THIN STRIPS)

1/4 CUP OLIVE OIL

1 CUP FINELY CHOPPED WHITE ONION
(FROM 1 1/2 TO 2 MEDIUM ONIONS)

1 TABLESPOON GROUND CUMIN

1 TABLESPOON PAPRIKA

1/2 TEASPOON CAYENNE PEPPER

1 TEASPOON GROUND CORIANDER

6 CUPS CHICKEN STOCK (PAGE 120)

4 MEDIUM GARLIC CLOVES, CRUSHED

4 CUPS CHOPPED TOMATOES

1 BAY LEAF

3 TABLESPOONS CHOPPED FRESH CILANTRO

2 BONELESS, SKINLESS CHICKEN BREASTS
(ABOUT 3/4 POUND)

1 TABLESPOON COARSE SEA SALT

1 LARGE RIPE HASS AVOCADO,
CUT INTO 1/2-INCH CUBES

1 CUP SHREDDED, AGED CHEDDAR

1/2 PINT SOUR CREAM, FOR GARNISH

1. Fill a large pot to a depth of 3 to 4 inches with vegetable oil. Heat the oil over medium-high heat until it reaches 350°F. The temperature of the oil should not exceed 375°F., nor should it begin to smoke. Once the oil is hot enough, lower the heat to medium. Add the tortilla strips and fry until crisp and golden, about 1 minute. Remove the strips with a skimmer or slotted spoon and drain well on paper towels.

2. Heat the olive oil in a large stockpot over medium-low flame. Add the onion, cumin, paprika, cayenne, coriander, and half the tortilla chips. Sauté for 8 to 10 minutes.

3. Add the stock, garlic, tomatoes, bay leaf, and 2 tablespoons of the chopped cilantro. Season the chicken breast with 1/2 tablespoon of the salt. Add to the pan with the remaining 1/2 tablespoon of salt. Reduce the heat to low and simmer for 1 hour.

4. Remove the chicken and bay leaf with a slotted spoon. When cool enough to handle, shred the chicken and set aside. Discard the bay leaf.

5. Purée 2 cups of the soup in a blender or food processor, taking care not to overload the bowl. Return the blended soup to the pot and continue cooking for an additional 2 minutes. (Or purée additional batches of soup, 2 cups at a time, depending upon your desired consistency—even purée all of it if you like.)

6. Transfer the soup to a large serving bowl and add the reserved shredded chicken, the avocado, cheese, and the remaining tablespoon of cilantro. Garnish with the reserved tortilla chips and sour cream and serve.

Red Snapper à la Veracruzana

I enjoy a mild, white-fleshed fish like red snapper, and I love to spice it up with a lively salsa of tomatoes, olives, and capers. This is my favorite type of Mexican cuisine: nothing heavy, no refried beans, no elaborate preparations or heavy sauces.

4 tablespoons extra-virgin olive oil

1 medium white onion, diced

4 garlic cloves, finely chopped

6 large tomatoes, peeled (see page 57) and chopped, or 1 28-ounce can whole tomatoes

1/4 cup white wine

24 large green olives, pitted and chopped

3 tablespoons capers, rinsed

3 pickled jalapeño peppers, chopped

1 teaspoon dried Mexican oregano (see Note)

1 teaspoon dried thymne

2 bay leaves

1 teaspoon coarse salt

1/2 teaspoon freshly ground black pepper

12 red snapper fillets (2 pounds total), skinless and picked over for small bones

1 teaspoon sugar

3 limes, cut into quarters, for garnish

1. Heat 2 tablespoons of the olive oil in a large sauté pan over medium-high flame. Add the onion and cook until golden, about 10 minutes. Add the garlic and cook for 2 more minutes. (Don't allow the garlic to burn; it will turn bitter.) Add the tomatoes and the wine, stir well, and cook for 10 minutes. Add the olives, capers, jalapeños, oregano, thyme, and bay leaves and stir well. Season with 1/2 teaspoon salt and 1/4 teaspoon pepper. Adjust the heat to low, partially cover the pan, and allow to simmer for 20 minutes.

2. Heat 1 tablespoon of the oil in a large cast-iron skillet or sauté pan over medium flame. Season the fish with the remaining salt and pepper and add the sugar. Sauté the fillets in batches of 4 for 2 minutes on each side. (The pan should be large enough to hold 4 of the fillets in a single layer with about 1 inch of space between them. Don't crowd the pan or the fish will steam instead of brown.) Add more oil if necessary before sautéing each new batch. Transfer the fish to a serving platter.

3. Pour the sauce over the fish, garnish the platter with lime wedges, and serve with Cilantro Rice (recipe follows) on the side.

NOTE Mexican oregano is stronger than the standard European or Greek variety; it can be found, dried, in most Hispanic markets.

911: Red Snapper

Place the fillets in a baking dish, pour the sauce on top, and bake them in the oven at 350°F. for 15 minutes. This is how you'll normally encounter fish *à la Veracruzana*; it's an acceptable strategy and result, although the fish does have a tendency to get soggy or mushy when baked.

911: Tortilla Soup

Buy a medium-size (7-ounce) bag of premade tortilla chips and break them into 1-inch pieces by hand.

Cilantro Rice

This dish is a lovely accompaniment for the fish; it features a delightfully fresh flavor and an equally appealing green tint. The slightly piquant flavor of cilantro helps highlight and turn up the volume on the fish and its pleasantly acidic sauce. Remember, a rice cooker is always a quick, easy alternative to preparing rice dishes in a pan on the stove; sauté the onion, then combine the ingredients in the rice cooker and follow the instructions supplied by the manufacturer. You can't go wrong.

2 tablespoons unsalted butter
1 medium white onion, finely chopped
2 cups converted white rice
3 cups Chicken Stock (page 120)
or Vegetable Stock
1 bunch of cilantro
(about 15 to 20 stalks), chopped
½ teaspoon coarse sea salt,
plus more to taste
Freshly ground black pepper, to taste

1. Preheat the oven to 350°F.
2. Melt the butter in a cast-iron pot over medium heat. Add the onion and cook until soft, about 2 minutes. Add the rice and stir until well coated, about 1 minute. Add the stock, cilantro, and ½ teaspoon salt, and bring to a boil. Cover the pot and place it in the oven for 20 minutes. Remove from the oven, allow to rest (covered) for 5 minutes, season with salt and pepper, and serve hot.

Ginger Flan

1 cup superfine sugar
2 cups whole milk
1 tablespoon chopped peeled fresh ginger
2 large eggs
4 large egg yolks

1. Preheat the oven to 275°F.
2. Combine 1 tablespoon of water with ½ cup of the sugar in a small saucepan and mix well. Over high heat, melt the sugar mixture until it turns a deep amber color. Add 1 additional tablespoon of cold water to stop the caramel from cooking. Transfer equal amounts of the caramel to six ramekins, coating the bottom of each one. Set aside.
3. Place the milk and ginger in a saucepan over high heat. Bring the mixture to a boil and remove immediately from the heat. In a medium bowl, combine the eggs, egg yolks, and the remaining sugar, and mix until smooth. Pour the milk-ginger mixture slowly into the egg-sugar mixture while stirring.
4. Pass the custard through a fine strainer or chinois and discard the foam. Divide equal portions of the custard among the six caramel-lined ramekins. Place a layer of newspaper in the bottom of an ovenproof glass gratin dish. Place the ramekins on the newspaper, add water to a level halfway up the ramekins, and place the glass dish in the oven. Bake for 40 to 45 minutes, until the custard has jelled. (It should jiggle a bit—but not run or slide—when shaken.) Remove the ramekins from the ovenproof dish, allow them to cool to room temperature, then refrigerate until the flan is cold, 1 to 2 hours.
5. To serve, run a knife around the inside edge of each ramekin to loosen the flan, then turn it over onto a plate. The flan can be served slightly chilled or allowed to warm up to room temperature, according to taste.

FOR PLATES AND BOWLS, THINK BIG

Using oversize plates and bowls makes a strong statement. It places the focus squarely on the food. It says that the chef is clearly unafraid to call attention to his or her creations, that there's nothing to hide and everything to celebrate. So don't be bashful: Serve your dinners on big plates and in oversize bowls!

411: The Bain-Marie

Leave it to the French to come up with a quaint, charming name for each and every cooking technique under the sun. A *bain-marie* can refer to any type of setup whereby a preparation is gently cooked or reheated when its cooking vessel is placed in hot water. A double boiler is one type of *bain-marie;* so are the large serving-warming dishes you see at cafeterias and catered events. In the case of this flan recipe, the *bain-marie* is a baking or gratin dish partially filled with water to distribute the heat in the ramekins during baking. Many recipes for loaves, flans, mousses, and similarly textured preparations call for this method. It's important not to allow the water to boil while baking custard; otherwise, condensation may fall back into the ramekins and ruin the custard's uniform, balanced texture, defeating the purpose of the whole exercise. The best way to accomplish this is to bring the water to a boil first, reduce the heat to a simmer, and then pour the water carefully into the *bain-marie.* Adding a layer of paper towel or newspaper to the bottom of a *bain-marie* for baking is recommended: it protects the custard from harsh heat.

Sex on the Beach
for 8

The Hamptons have some of the best beaches I've seen anywhere in the world, yet they're only two to three hours east of New York City. Which is why every summer weekend we witness a mass exodus in the direction of that paradise. For a special treat, I planned a clambake for a quiet weeknight and found a pristine beach in the village of East Hampton where you felt you could really touch the sea and the sky. Late afternoon and evening are simply magical at this time of year in this place. I try to give at least one beach party per year and—with all the dinners I put together —it may be *the* annual highlight. It's certainly the ultimate picnic, and I look forward to it longingly all year round.

As a dining enclave, I created a kind of tent from two white umbrellas placed side-by-side with mosquito netting draped between them. I set up a low table using milk crates and a large piece of plywood. For dinner, we all sat around it on the sand, Roman-style. The color scheme was simple khaki and white— ephemeral, shifting the focus to the incredible natural ambience. The setting is preternaturally quiet and romantic; you commune with nature and you enjoy a simple, delicious meal in the company of good friends. Our voices seemed to carry for miles; the only other sounds were the gentle splashing of the waves and the occasional cry of a seagull.

For the menu, I turned to a local seafood shop and catering operation called Claws on Wheels. Over the years, they've perfected a technique for creating a clambake in one large pot. It consists of five fresh, local ingredients—mussels, clams, lobsters, potatoes, and corn—steamed and served piping hot with plenty of butter for dipping on the side. With Claws on Wheels, you have several options: Buy the ingredients, prepare the clambake, and cook it yourself; buy the clambake prepared and simply cook it; or hire them to do it all, start to finish. The seafood shop is run by Chris Minardi, whose dad, Tony, the founder, now runs the busy Claws on Wheels catering operation next door. It serves all of Long Island and is capable of putting together clambakes for intimate or very large parties.

The Menu: Supper for Eight

The Clambake
Mussels, Clams, Lobsters, Potatoes, and Corn

Dessert
Key Lime Pie

To Drink
Cocktail de Nuit: Sex on the Beach

Assorted beers on ice

Good summer white wines
in a large galvanized steel tub or cooler. Your best bet is a rich Chardonnay with tropical fruit character and a hint of French country butter, which goes so well with the lobster. The wine should also maintain enough acidity to keep it refreshing. Try the Lewis Sonoma Chardonnay or some equally delicious white.

Sex on the Beach

TIMING Set up the clambake well before the guests arrive and place the pot on the fire just before their arrival. While the ice melts and you are waiting for the ingredients to begin steaming, serve cocktails (the clambake should take about an hour to reach the boiling point). If you choose to prepare a wood fire, light it an hour or two before you plan to start heating the pot, and stoke it well.

Here is one recipe that requires very little explanation. Whether or not you reveal its name from the outset, this cocktail will put your guests in the proper mood for . . . anything! Fresh juices are always preferable, but if you use bottled ones, make sure they are of the best quality.

4 ounces black raspberry liqueur

4 ounces melon liqueur

4 ounces vodka

8 ounces pineapple juice

1 12-ounce bottle cranberry juice

Fill a large cocktail shaker or pitcher with ice. Add the black raspberry liqueur, melon liqueur, vodka, and pineapple juice, and stir well. Strain equal amounts of the mixture into chilled glasses, top with cranberry juice, and consume immediately.

CLAMBAKE

One of the great things about this clambake technique is that you can prepare the pot back at the house, put it in the back of an SUV or wagon, drive it down to the beach, and have plenty of time to set up. The ingredients are kept fresh on ice until you put the pot on the fire, the ice begins to melt, and they start to steam.

Be sure to provide an extra pot or several large dishes for discarding the clam, mussel, and lobster shells. Also, in addition to standard table utensils, don't forget to provide crackers for the lobster claws. I find it's also helpful to set up a sturdy table with a cutting board and to crack the lobster claws with a small hammer before putting them on each plate.

Show some respect and consideration for the environment: Use cloth napkins and inexpensive stainless-steel flatware, rather than the throwaways. Bring large garbage and recycling bags, and pick up everything before you leave the beach at the end of the evening.

4 DOZEN MEDIUM-SIZE MUSSELS,
RINSED WELL AND BEARDS REMOVED

4 DOZEN LITTLENECK CLAMS
(2 TO 3 INCHES IN DIAMETER), RINSED WELL

8 LOBSTERS (1 1/4 TO 1 1/2 POUNDS EACH)

8 EARS OF CORN, OUTER HUSKS REMOVED,
INNER HUSKS LEFT ON, ENDS TRIMMED OFF AND HALVED

16 MEDIUM RED POTATOES, QUARTERED
(OR 3 TO 4 DOZEN NEW RED POTATOES)

1 5-POUND BAG OF ICE CUBES

1 TO 2 POUNDS UNSALTED BUTTER

4 LEMONS, QUARTERED, FOR GARNISH

1. In the pot place the following ingredients in layers in this order (starting from the bottom): mussels, clams, lobsters, corn, potatoes. Do not pack the layers down; simply lay the ingredients in the pot. The mussels and clams should cover the entire bottom of the pot, insulating the lobsters from coming in contact with the bottom. Otherwise, the lobsters can become soggy and taste watery.

2. Pour the equivalent of about two large icemaker scoops (about 2 quarts) of ice cubes from the 5-pound bag into the pot, allowing the ice to fill all the gaps. The ice cubes should fill the pot nearly to the top, leaving just enough room to cover it tightly. (You can reserve the remainder of the bag in a cooler for drinks.)

3. Cover the pot and place it on a propane gas burner or a wood fire over high heat. (Note: Electric burners can work for clambakes, but they take much longer; grills do not work.) The 8-person clambake should take about 1 hour for the pot to steam, depending on the strength of your fire. Larger clambakes take longer to reach the boiling point. Once the pot is steaming, allow it to continue for another 15 minutes if the lobsters are 1 1/4-pounders, or 18 to 20 minutes if the lobsters are 1 1/2-pounders. Check the layer of potatoes on top of the pot; when they are tender, the entire clambake is done.

4. While the clambake is steaming, melt the butter in a saucepan and keep it warm. (Or simply place the saucepan on the lid of the pot; there is plenty of heat to melt the butter.)

5. When the clambake is done, remove the pot from the fire (or turn off the burner). Using a large slotted spoon and/or a set of tongs, serve half a dozen each of the mussels and clams, 1 lobster, a portion of potatoes, two half-ears of corn, and 2 lemon quarters per plate. (Larger clambakes can be served either cafeteria style or as a buffet).

KEY LIME PIE

There are about as many recipes for Key lime pie as there are chefs who prepare it, and of course each one proudly proclaims his or her recipe as the best. This one is among my favorites. It's about as easy as they come, and there's no question as to its authenticity since it comes from the producers of Nellie & Joe's Famous Lime Juice in Key West, Florida. Since there are a lot of other details to be attended to with the clambake, I suggest you buy the pie crust; however, you can also make one, and I provide the recipe below.

At the clambake, we served each slice of pie with a refreshing treat: generous wedge of seedless watermelon. The folks at Nellie & Joe's recommend serving fresh whipped cream (see page 109) and slices of lime as a garnish—and I agree wholeheartedly.

1 14-OUNCE CAN SWEETENED CONDENSED MILK

3 LARGE EGG YOLKS

1/2 CUP NELLIE & JOE'S FAMOUS LIME JUICE

1 9-INCH PIE CRUST (RECIPE FOLLOWS)

1. Preheat the oven to 350°F.

2. Combine the condensed milk, egg yolks, and lime juice in a large bowl (see Note) and stir vigorously until the mixture is smooth.

3. Pour the filling into the pie crust and bake for 10 minutes. Remove from the oven and allow to cool for 10 minutes before refrigerating a minimum of 1 hour.

PIE CRUST

2 CUPS ALL-PURPOSE FLOUR

⅛ TEASPOON SALT

1 STICK (½ CUP) UNSALTED BUTTER,
THINLY SLICED AND FROZEN

1 EGG, BEATEN

1. Place the flour, salt, and butter in the bowl of a food processor fitted with the metal blade. Pulse until well combined, 4 to 6 times. Switch the processor to continuous operation and add 6 tablespoons of water until the dough forms a ball. Remove the dough ball from the food processor, flatten it into a disk, wrap it in plastic, and refrigerate for at least 1 hour.

2. Preheat the oven to 350°F.

3. Roll out the dough on a lightly floured board to a thickness of ¼ inch. Line the bottom of a 10-inch springform pan with the dough, trimming the edges so they don't overlap the sides of the pan. Brush the inside of the dough with the beaten egg, pierce it all over with a fork, and line it with foil. Fill the pan with uncooked beans to weight the crust and bake for 20 minutes. Set the crust aside to cool, then proceed with step 3 of the recipe above.

NOTE You can combine the milk, egg yolks, and lime juice in a food processor, instead of a large bowl, if you prefer.

411: Equipment Checklist

Large pot or pots, big enough to fit all the ingredients in layers plus room to spare for ice (the 4-person clambake requires a 10-gallon pot; the 8-person clambake, a 20-gallon pot)

Potholders

Propane burner(s) or wood fire

Hammer and crackers for cracking lobster shells

Large serving plates

Saucepan for melting butter

Serving dishes or bowls for butter

Serving utensils: large slotted spoons and large tongs

Table utensils, glasses, plates, napkins

Folding table(s) for serving/buffet

Milk crates and a piece of plywood for the dining table

Tiki torches and other candles, with candelabras

Blankets, sheets, or light rugs for spreading on the sand

Bug repellant coils and spray

Extra dishes or containers for shells, recyclables, and other refuse

Roll of paper towels, Handi Wipes, and several large (30-gallon) trash bags

411: Per-Person Portions

Ours was a relatively small clambake for 8. Most clambakes are larger. Here are some guidelines for purchasing the basic ingredients on a per-person basis:

- Mussels and clams: half a dozen

- Lobsters: one 1¼- to 1½-pounder

- Potatoes: one medium red potato or four new red potatoes

- Corn: one or two ears (depending on their size)

In the Vineyard
for 10

So much of our time is spent indoors that when summer arrives it's really a treat to dine out under the stars. Of course, if you're fortunate enough to live in southern California or some other place with an equally pleasant climate, you can dine alfresco almost year round. It's a pleasure I never take for granted—especially now that I spend so much time in Manhattan. In this case, we were invited to make ourselves at home at the house of my close friend Kevin Wendle, located on a beautiful property in the hills of Bel Air.

I wanted the evening to be casual, rustic, and relaxed. The idea was to create a communal feast centered around a table laden abundantly with plates of hearty country-style food that would transport our guests to the Mediterranean. It wouldn't be much of a stretch to imagine they were somewhere in Provence or Tuscany, overlooking a vineyard with grapevines hanging from the trellises all around.

The tableware is a wonderful combination of terra-cotta pieces and wooden boards. Since we were dining outdoors, Italian style, I used tumblers instead of stemmed, footed wineglasses. Everything was geared toward making this an informal, inviting feast, the kind of meal at which you feel absolutely no hesitation to soak up the scrumptious swirling sauces on your plate with a good crusty chunk of peasant bread.

Although the meal is quite multifaceted, you'll be buying most of the items for the appetizer course in the store and thereby saving a lot of prep time. To avoid aggravation and to make it a thoroughly enjoyable experience, write up a good list before you shop. Then give yourself some leeway when you get to the cheese and charcuterie counters. If a particular item looks too good to resist—if it really talks to you—don't hesitate to buy it and find a place for it on your table. You might discover something wonderful.

For the first course, I assembled a stunning board of delicacies, lining the center of the table with plates of different types of salamis and prosciutto, bowls of assorted olives, country breads, fresh figs, cornichons. . . . You can really let your enthusiasm carry you as far as you like. I stuck to a country theme—part Provençal, part Tuscan—but feel free to go farther afield if you like. The goal is to generate a sense of abundance, that aura of warm country hospitality and gracious generosity. It's all about celebrating the bountiful harvest and rejoicing in the fruits of the earth, a ritual performed with revelry and delight in cultures the world over.

For place cards, I used a full head of garlic at each place setting. Not only did this indicate to the guests where they should sit, but it also announced in no uncertain terms the tone and energy of the occasion: rustic and inviting. Furthermore, it provided an enticing preview of the scrumptious garlic-based main course to come.

THE MENU: SUPPER FOR TEN

APPETIZER PLATES
CHEESE PLATE, ASSORTED OLIVES WITH CORNICHONS
FOIE GRAS IN A CAST-IRON POT

MAIN COURSE
CHICKEN AND THE FORTY CLOVES
WHITE BEANS WITH PANCETTA

DESSERT
CHOCOLATE POT DE CRÈME

TO DRINK
COCKTAIL DE NUIT: PERNOD WITH MINERAL WATER
WINE: ROSÉ
THE WINE FOR THE ENTIRE MEAL WAS DOMAINE OTT ROSÉ,
A DELICIOUS AND VERSATILE WINE FROM PROVENCE, EXCELLENT
FOR WARM-WEATHER MEALS. IT WORKED EQUALLY WELL WITH
THE APPETIZER COURSE AND THE MAIN DISH.

TIMING This is a meal that requires some advance preparation, so it's best to plan it for a weekend. If you're feeling a little more ambitious, it can be done on a weeknight, but be sure to perform a few key steps either the night before or the morning of the party. The foie gras, should you choose to make it, needs to be refrigerated for at least 8 hours. The beans need to be soaked overnight in advance. The dessert takes about 2 hours total, including at least an hour of cooling in the fridge. Everything can be done in advance. The main dish is a simple one-pot preparation that can bubble away in the oven while you're setting the table, laying out the appetizer buffet, and making other last-minute arrangements.

Pernod and Mineral Water

Pernod is a descendant of the infamous liqueur absinthe (a.k.a. wormwood), which fueled many poets and artists of the late nineteenth and early twentieth centuries. Absinthe was extremely potent (136 proof, or 68 percent alcohol), tasted of anise, and was considered both an aphrodisiac and a hallucinogen. It was often served by pouring it through a small strainer or slotted spoon containing sugar to balance its powerful bitterness. Because of its addictive properties and the nerve damage it caused among heavy users, absinthe was outlawed in the early twentieth century. If you're naughty, I understand you can find bars that still pour the stuff . . .

Pernod, named for the first commercial distiller of absinthe, is a milder drink now flavored with aniseed. Authentically Mediterranean, the anise flavor is an acquired taste but is definitely worth a try. Aniseed is also used to flavor the Greek liqueur ouzo, which is also traditionally served as an apéritif, and its Turkish equivalent, raki, as well as the Italian versions anisette and Sambuca. All these drinks turn white when you mix them with water, which is quite necessary due to their potency.

For a Pernod and water, simply pour 1½ to 2 ounces of Pernod into a rocks glass or highball glass with ice and top it off with still (bottled) mineral water. The proportion of Pernod to water should be 1 to 4 or 1 to 5.

APPETIZERS

The foie gras is the featured recipe in this appetizer buffet. The rest of the delicacies (cheese, bread, olives, cornichons, and whatever else suits your fancy) are store-bought prepared items. If you don't want to go to the trouble of preparing the foie gras yourself, you can simply buy a *pâté de foie gras* (duck-liver paté) or some other type of *terrine*.

CHEESE PLATE

In keeping with the character of this meal, you'll want to serve some substantial rustic or country-style cheeses. I chose an assorted plate of five French and Italian cheeses: Saint-André, Morbier, Taleggio, Parmigiano-Reggiano, and Gorgonzola. If you prefer to lean more to the French side, try substituting a Reblochon and a Tomme de Savoie for the Taleggio and Gorgonzola. If you decide to take a more Italian tack, you might want to substitute a Pecorino for the Morbier; in any case, be sure to select a genuine aged Parmesan and a mature, ripe Taleggio. For an authentic Tuscan touch, simply serve a fine aged Pecorino Toscano with raw shelled fava beans. (The best versions of this superb sheep's-milk cheese come from the area around the town of Pienza in south-central Tuscany, and are labeled Pecorino di Pienza.) The contrast between the fresh, green, crunchy beans and the smooth, rich, nutty cheese is truly sublime. Other delicious accompaniments for a fine Pecorino are honey, dried fruit, and walnuts.

Saint-André, by the way, is one of the sensuous, opulent French *triple-crème* cheeses that are made from milk enriched with extra cream. The triple-crèmes contain no less than 75 percent butterfat, which sounds like an awful lot. Actually, since they are softer cheeses with higher water content, they can have less fat per solid weight than a harder cheese with a lower percentage of butterfat, such as Parmesan. (Butterfat is listed as a percentage relative to solid matter; Parmesan has about 35 percent butterfat.) Saint-André comes from the Rouergue zone of south-central France. The other most famous triple-crèmes are Brillat-Savarin and Explorateur.

411: Cheese

I'm as passionate about cheese as I am about any other category of food. For a continental after-dinner cheese plate, I go for a selection of at least five and possibly as many as seven different cheeses. I try to alternate sheep's-, goat's-, and cow's-milk selections and strive to offer a good balance of hard and soft, delicate and powerful, mild and strong, with at least one blue cheese. I place them in ascending order from the mildest to the strongest.

When serving cheese as part of an appetizer buffet, I recommend limiting the number to three or four. You'll be serving nothing but the finest, most irresistible cheeses, of course, so you don't want your guests to fill up too much before the main course.

An important note on serving cheeses: Always serve them at room temperature, not cold straight out of the refrigerator. Allow 1 to 1½ hours out of the fridge before serving. Cold masks a large percentage of a cheese's flavors and aromas.

FOIE GRAS IN A CAST-IRON POT

Like most of the recipes in this book, this is a simple, straightforward version, but it does need to be prepared far enough in advance so that it can rest in the fridge for a good 8 hours. You might choose to do it the night before or in the morning before you go about your day's business.

1 1/2 POUNDS FRESH VACUUM-PACKED FOIE GRAS
(DUCK LIVER)
2 TEASPOONS COARSE SEA SALT,
PLUS ENOUGH TO FILL A BOWL (SEE NOTE)
1 TEASPOON FRESHLY GROUND BLACK PEPPER
TOASTED BREAD OR CRISPY CROUTONS

1. Preheat the oven to 400°F.
2. Remove the foie gras from its package and pat it dry using a paper towel. Remove any green veins or nerves or lumps from the exterior of the liver by scraping it lightly with a paring knife. Season it with the salt and pepper.
3. Heat a cast-iron pot or other heavy-bottomed pot over high flame until very hot. Add the duck liver and quickly brown it on two sides, approximately 5 seconds each side. Remove the pot from the heat and cover.
4. Place the pot with the foie gras in the oven for 10 to 15 minutes. (The rule of thumb is 10 minutes per pound.) Remove the pot from the oven, allow it to cool, then place it in the refrigerator for at least 8 hours. This allows the foie gras to set and Its flavors to meld, transforming it into a sliceable, spreadable loaf.
5. To serve, remove the liver from the pot and place it on a cutting board. Season with coarse sea salt. Serve with toast or crispy croutons.

NOTE Serve a bowl of coarse sea salt alongside the foie gras; it helps cut the dense richness of the liver and adds a crunchy texture contrast to the dish. In summer, serve foie gras with fresh figs.

CHICKEN AND THE FORTY CLOVES

Here's an old French peasant recipe that I've enjoyed for years. It's an unbelievably delicious and deceptively plain dish that is brought directly from the oven to the table, piping hot and exquisitely aromatic. It's best prepared in a clay pot, leaving the top uncovered for the last 15 minutes so it can brown. The best way to eat it is with hearty peasant bread to soak up the mouth-watering sauce. But first squeeze the roasted garlic cloves so their flesh pops out of the skin and spread them on the bread; garlic mellows nicely when it's roasted. To make this into a complete meal, add 16 baby potatoes to the pot after 1 hour of cooking. They'll simmer in the hot broth and will be loaded with flavor by the time the chicken is done.

2 WHOLE CHICKENS
(APPROXIMATELY 3 1/2 POUNDS EACH)

2 TABLESPOONS COARSE SEA SALT,
PLUS MORE TO TASTE

1 TABLESPOON FRESHLY GROUND BLACK PEPPER

4 SPRIGS OF FRESH THYME

4 SPRIGS OF FRESH ROSEMARY

4 SPRIGS OF FRESH SAGE

4 CELERY STALKS (WITH THE LEAVES)

4 SPRIGS OF FRESH FLAT-LEAF PARSLEY

40 GARLIC CLOVES, UNPEELED

2 TABLESPOONS OLIVE OIL

1 CUP CHICKEN STOCK (PAGE 120)

1. Preheat the oven to 400°F.

2. Season the chicken cavities with half of the salt and pepper. Stuff them with half of the thyme, rosemary, sage, celery, parsley, and 8 cloves of garlic for each bird. Place the remaining herbs and celery in the bottom of a clay or cast-iron pot large enough to hold both chickens. Add the chickens to the pot, coat them evenly with the oil, then season with the remaining salt and pepper. Add the remaining garlic and the chicken stock to the pot, cover, and bake for 80 minutes, basting every 20 minutes.

3. Uncover the pot, season with salt to taste, and continue baking until the chicken skin is crispy, its juices run clear, and its internal temperature is 175°F., another 15 minutes. (This uncovered step is optional; it depends on how you like your chicken.)

4. Transfer the cooked chickens to a serving platter and surround them with the cloves of garlic. Skim the fat from the cooking juices using a large flat spoon or ladle, and pour the juices into a sauceboat. Serve the chicken with the hot sauce.

WHITE BEANS WITH PANCETTA

Beans are the ultimate comfort food. White beans are a little more subtle in flavor, texture, and appearance than their red or black cousins. Yet they retain plenty of that rustic feel to match this meal. Pancetta is Italian salt-cured (unsmoked) bacon—another inexpensive country item that has become a staple of sophisticated cuisine. You can substitute a standard smoked bacon.

4 CUPS DRY WHITE BEANS
(NAVY, GREAT NORTHERN, OR CANNELLINI), SOAKED FOR A MINIMUM OF 4 HOURS (PREFERABLY OVERNIGHT) IN COLD WATER

1/2 POUND PANCETTA OR SMOKED BACON, DICED

2 CUPS DICED CELERY
(FROM ABOUT 4 MEDIUM STALKS)

2 CUPS DICED ONION
(FROM 4 MEDIUM ONIONS, ABOUT I POUND)

2 CUPS DICED CARROTS (FROM ABOUT 2/3 POUND)

4 GARLIC CLOVES, CRUSHED

2 BOUQUETS GARNIS (SEE NOTE, PAGE I 20)

I 1/2 TABLESPOONS SALT, PLUS MORE TO TASTE

I TABLESPOON FRESHLY GROUND BLACK PEPPER,
PLUS MORE TO TASTE

4 TABLESPOONS EXTRA-VIRGIN OLIVE OIL

I TABLESPOON CHOPPED FRESH FLAT-LEAF PARSLEY

911: Quick-Soaked Beans

What to do if you forgot to soak the beans overnight? After being picked through and rinsed, beans have traditionally been soaked overnight at room temperature in enough water to cover them by about 2 inches. Some bean experts now advocate a quicker "hot-soaking" method: Place the beans in a large saucepan or stockpot with 1 quart of water for each cup of beans. Bring the water to a boil over high heat, cook for about 2 minutes, remove the pot from the heat, and allow the beans to soak and swell in the pot for 1 hour. Then simply follow the regular recipe directions.

The reason we presoak beans is to reduce their infamous gas-producing properties. Beans contain many complex sugar molecules, which are indigestible in the human stomach. If the beans are not presoaked, these sugars make their way into the intestines. There, local bacteria consume them and give off their well-known by-product: noxious gasses.

1. Drain and rinse the beans.
2. Place the pancetta, celery, onions, and carrots in a large pot over medium-high heat and cook for 5 minutes, until the vegetables and pancetta are lightly browned. Add the garlic, drained beans, bouquets garnis, and enough water to cover the beans by 1 inch. Partially cover the pot and lower the heat to a simmer.
3. After 30 minutes, season the beans with the salt and pepper, then return the lid to partially cover the pot again. Cook for an additional 30 minutes, until the beans are creamy and tender.
4. Transfer the beans to a platter, drizzle with the olive oil, top with parsley, and sprinkle with freshly ground pepper. Serve.

CHOCOLATE POT DE CRÈME

Pot de crème is essentially a crème brûlée without the caramelized top. (In restaurants, they caramelize it with a blowtorch.) It's a wonderful, rich cream custard. In this case, I made it with good old-fashioned bittersweet chocolate, but it also works well with white chocolate or vanilla. I like to serve these little delicacies in espresso cups; that way, the portions are just the right size, and one can really appreciate the flavors and textures without overdoing it on the fat and sugar front.

1 CUP HEAVY CREAM

½ CUP WHOLE MILK

4 OUNCES GOOD-QUALITY DARK CHOCOLATE,
COARSELY CHOPPED

4 EGG YOLKS

¼ CUP SUGAR

1. Preheat the oven to 325°F.

2. Bring the cream and milk to a slow boil in a small pot over high heat. Remove from the heat immediately and transfer to a large mixing bowl. Add the chocolate and whisk until the mixture is smooth and all the chocolate is melted. Set aside to cool.

3. In a medium mixing bowl, whisk the egg yolks and sugar until smooth but not foamy. Gradually combine the cooled chocolate mixture and the egg mixture in the large mixing bowl, stirring constantly. Strain the combined mixture through a fine sieve and pour into individual espresso cups.

4. Line the bottom of an ovenproof glass dish (large enough to hold all the espresso cups) with newspaper for proper heat transfer. Transfer the cups to the dish and fill it two-thirds full with hot water. Bake for 35 to 40 minutes, until the custard has set. Remove from the oven, allow to cool to room temperature, then place the cups in the refrigerator for at least 1 hour before serving. Serve with the garnish or accompaniment of your choice: Try fresh raspberries and whipped cream, confectioners' sugar, caramel ice cream, or cocoa powder.

CELADON CHIC
FOR 4

Sometimes, the layout and decor of a space will really talk to me, and when it does I'm often inspired to celebrate. In this case, it was the apartment of my good friend and fellow South African, the gifted interior designer Geoffrey Bradfield.

Geoffrey's place is stunning—simple, clean, elegant, uncluttered, and well edited. (And, as we all know, when it comes to any type of design, well-edited is the best.) Geoffrey's interior design for the apartment is based on the Art Moderne style, more commonly known as Art Deco. It began in the 1920s, was in full swing in the thirties and forties, and is integral to much of New York City's finest architecture, interior and exterior. The building, formerly the Mayfair Hotel, is a sixteen-story Gothic-revival apartment house at Park Avenue and Sixty-fifth Street in Manhattan. The sleek lines, sweeping curves, geometrical patterns, and subtle color variations of Art Deco are just right for a renovation in this setting. The apartment space is reminiscent of a forties movie set—I could see Cary Grant or Carole Lombard striding confidently through the doorway at any moment—but is equally appropriate for a contemporary fast-paced urban lifestyle.

There is an indelibly soothing feel to the apartment's slightly retro ambience. It brings on a sense of calm, which is always welcome at the end of a hectic day. The color scheme consists of various shades of light green, including mint, pistachio (notice these are both food colors!), and particularly celadon. These elements spurred me to create a dinner party based on fresh, pure, unadorned ingredients. The color theme was initiated by the use of celadon in the custom carpet and in several pieces of the furniture. I took off on a tangent, introducing other shades of green from avocado to chartreuse.

The green color theme runs throughout the meal, beginning with the Sour-Apple Martini, whose marvelous shade of pale green is accentuated by an elegant, paper-thin slice of green apple. There's more light green in the avocado and fennel of the first-course salad and later in the pistachio ice cream. I love the way colors can subliminally affect the mood of an occasion. (Have you ever wondered why they paint so many fast-food restaurants yellow and red?) Green is a vibrant, refreshing color; pale shades of it are relaxing, calming, and meditative.

Concentrating on a Color Scheme

The dictionary definition of *celadon* is a delicate color of pale grayish green. It's an ephemeral color, mellow and soothing—a far cry from hot pink or raucous red. When you say "pale green," that's a bit pedestrian; but call it "celadon" and it adds the flavors of romance, intrigue, and mystery. It's suggestive, languidly sensual.

When you pick a color scheme and stick with it in this way, it becomes like a leitmotiv (or recurring theme) in music or literature. Each time it returns to the forefront of our consciousness, it gives a sense of coordination, planning, integration; it reinforces the notion that there's a higher intelligence (or at least an overall vision) at work, that the meal and the whole occasion isn't just thrown together in a haphazard or carelessly eclectic manner. It's an inconspicuous way of saying this is a planned occasion, not a slapdash picnic or last-minute takeout meal.

This was an intimate gathering for a light, early dinner. The occasion was suited to going out afterward for a night on the town or simply relaxing, retiring early, and getting a good night's sleep. The meal itself took on a restrained, elegant aesthetic in keeping with the apartment's design theme. None of the dishes is overly heavy, so you could easily go to the theater without having to worry about nodding off halfway through the performance. (Plus, we ended the meal with a good strong cup of espresso.)

Other than the two white seventeenth-century elephants (incense holders that were used as candelabras), everything in the place was from the 1940s or later. For the center of the table, I created a streamlined flower arrangement by packing two julep cups tightly with viburnum, which is light and simple and has a fresh, very spring-like look to it. To add an element of illumination, I provided pearlized oversized sphere-shaped candles for the seventeenth-century incense holders.

APPETIZER
FENNEL-AVOCADO SALAD

MAIN COURSE
HALIBUT EN PAPILLOTE
NEW POTATOES

DESSERT
PEARS POACHED IN RED WINE
WITH PISTACHIO ICE CREAM
SHORTBREAD COOKIES

TO DRINK
COCKTAIL DE NUIT: SOUR-APPLE MARTINI
WINE: WHITE BURGUNDY
SUCH AS PULIGNY-MONTRACHET OR CORTON-CHARLEMAGNE

TIMING The poached pears need to be made a day in advance. The salad can be prepared in advance of the guests' arrival and dressed just before serving, which is the great thing about almost any salad. The fish packets for the main course can also be entirely prepped in advance and then popped in the oven either before or during the salad course, depending upon your timing instincts and how the dinner is proceeding. The cookies for dessert are optional; they can be made in advance or bought in a store.

SOUR-APPLE MARTINI

I've hosted many a memorable party that began with this stunning cocktail. It's certainly one drink that looks as good as it tastes. Be sure to save the ginger ale for last—don't shake it in the shaker. Otherwise, the carbonation is liable to blow the lid off, which would start the party off with a little too much of a bang!

Remember, green is our theme. So for cocktail munchies, I suggest pistachios. (The Iranian ones are the best.)

6 OUNCES VODKA
3 OUNCES SOUR-APPLE SCHNAPPS
1 TEASPOON LIME JUICE
3 OUNCES GINGER ALE
4 PAPER-THIN CROSS-SECTION SLICES OF GREEN APPLE

1. Chill 4 martini glasses (see page 181).
2. Place the vodka, schnapps, and lime juice in a shaker full of ice. Shake vigorously, then strain into the chilled glasses, leaving enough room in each for a shy ounce of ginger ale. Top each glass with ginger ale, garnish with a slice of apple, and serve.

FENNEL-AVOCADO SALAD

I aimed to create something light and elegant with as little fuss as possible. This salad, with hearts of palm, fennel, and avocado, certainly fit the bill. And color-wise, it provided several delightful shades of light green. I call for the fennel to be sliced with a mandoline, the classic French mechanism for ultimate precision in carving up your firm vegetables, but a very sharp grater or kitchen knife can be used. Just be sure to slice the fennel as thin as possible; otherwise, its licorice-like flavor tends to overwhelm the subtler flavors in this salad, such as the avocado and hearts of palm.

1 FENNEL BULB,
SLICED PAPER-THIN WITH A MANDOLINE
OR VERY SHARP KITCHEN KNIFE

2 EGGS, HARD-BOILED, PEELED AND QUARTERED
(SEE NOTE)

1 4-OUNCE LOG OF GOAT CHEESE, THINLY SLICED

1 BUNCH OF RADISHES, THINLY SLICED

2 HEADS OF FRISÉE, WASHED AND DRIED

2 AVOCADOS, PEELED, PITTED,
AND CUT INTO ¼- TO ½-INCH CUBES

3 HEARTS OF PALM, SLICED ¼- TO ½-INCH THICK

LEMON VINAIGRETTE (RECIPE FOLLOWS)

2 TABLESPOONS FINELY CHOPPED CHIVES, FOR GARNISH

411: The Magnificent Avocado

This tropical treasure, renowned for its smooth, unctuous texture and subtle, ambrosial flavor, is technically a fruit. (In case you were wondering, the name comes from the word for testicle in one of the ancient Central American languages.) Avocados come in a variety of shapes and sizes: The two most popular types are Hass, which has a thicker, darker, rough-textured skin, and Fuerte, which has a thinner, greener skin. Like pears, avocados ripen well off the tree. Most of them are grown in California and shipped all over the country. If you need to speed up their ripening, just store them in a paper bag at room temperature for two or three days. Avocados should be cut as close to serving time as possible since they will go dark with exposure to air. You can also sprinkle them with lemon juice to prevent discoloration.

1. **Combine all the salad ingredients in a large salad bowl, add the vinaigrette, and toss well. Sprinkle with the chopped chives and serve.**

NOTE To hard-boil eggs, place them in a small saucepan of boiling water, lower the heat to a simmer, and cook for 6 to 8 minutes. In order to serve the eggs cold immediately, plunge them into a bath of ice water for up to 5 minutes before peeling.

LEMON VINAIGRETTE

1 TABLESPOON DIJON MUSTARD

¼ CUP FRESH LEMON JUICE
(ABOUT 5 TABLESPOONS, FROM 2 MEDIUM LEMONS)

½ CUP EXTRA-VIRGIN OLIVE OIL

¼ TEASPOON SALT

⅛ TEASPOON FRESHLY GROUND BLACK PEPPER

Place the mustard and lemon juice in a blender or food processor and pulse until well mixed. Gradually add the oil while processing until the mixture emulsifies. Season with salt and pepper.

I enjoy food that has an element of theater. I've always been partial to moments of ceremony—the show of opening a wine bottle, or individually hand-serving a poached egg for the top of a salad, or ladling a piping-hot portion of steamed mussels into a bowl. I like to bring these fish packets to the table like little gifts, creating a "moment" when each guest pulls apart the wrapper to reveal the delicious steaming contents with a positively ambrosial aroma. Cooking any kind of food—particularly fish, which starts out moist but has a delicate flesh very prone to drying out—in a package is a sure-fire way to ensure tender consistency and a complete melding of flavors.

¼ CUP PLUS 1 TABLESPOON OLIVE OIL

1 POUND BABY SPINACH, WASHED AND DRIED

1 TEASPOON PLUS 1 PINCH SALT

½ TEASPOON PLUS 1 PINCH FRESHLY GROUND
BLACK PEPPER

4 MEDIUM RIPE TOMATOES, PEELED
(SEE PAGE 57), SEEDED, AND DICED

2 TABLESPOONS SMALL CAPERS, DRAINED AND RINSED

¼ CUP CHOPPED FRESH BASIL

¼ CUP COARSELY CHOPPED KALAMATA
OR CURED BLACK OLIVES

2 TABLESPOONS BALSAMIC VINEGAR

4 7-OUNCE FILLETS OF HALIBUT,
SKINLESS AND BONELESS

1 LEMON, THINLY SLICED, FOR GARNISH

1. Preheat the oven to 350°F.

2. Heat 1 tablespoon of the olive oil in a large skillet over medium flame. Add the spinach and sauté for 1 minute. Remove from the heat, season with a pinch each of salt and pepper, and set aside. (Alternatively, you can drop the spinach in a pot of boiling, salted water for 5 seconds, then remove it immediately and drain it thoroughly in a colander.) Once it's cool, squeeze the excess water from the spinach.

3. In a medium bowl, combine the tomatoes, capers, basil, olives, remaining ½ cup of olive oil, and the vinegar. Set aside.

4. Cut out 4 pieces of parchment paper, each approximately 11 × 14 inches. Drizzle olive oil on the paper, place an equal portion of the reserved spinach in the center of each, and lay a piece of halibut on top. Spoon equal portions of the tomato mixture on each piece of fish to make a neat mound of ingredients in the center of each sheet of parchment paper. Season the fish with the 1 teaspoon of salt and the ½ teaspoon of pepper.

(continued on page 174)

Getting the Most Bang for Your Buck

I like to get as much payoff as possible from the smallest investment. A recipe such as this Halibut en Papillote is an excellent example: The preparations can be done in an hour or less; the dish looks great and tastes equally fabulous; and it's not something you eat every day. Your guests will definitely be impressed, not in the sense of one-upmanship, but because you've taken the time to share your hospitality and serve them a memorable and delicious meal.

5. Fold the bottom third of each sheet over its mound of ingredients. Then fold the top third back down on top of the bottom third. Next, fold a 1-inch strip of the top third back on top of itself. Finally, tuck the left and right sides snugly under the mound to secure the packet.

6. Place the packets of fish on a baking sheet and bake for 15 to 20 minutes. The packets are done when the fish, visible through the parchment, has just turned white. Remove the baking sheet from the oven and allow the packets to stand for 5 minutes before opening. Slip the slices of lemon into the folds of the packets before bringing them to the table. Place a fish packet on each plate and allow each of your guests to open his or her own packet. Serve with new potatoes on the side.

New Potatoes

New potatoes are simply young ones of any variety. There's something to be said for youth—even in a vegetable. For this recipe, you can use the small versions of either white round or red round potatoes. They are elegant, mild, fresh, even slightly sweet, and they lend themselves well to beautiful presentation.

12 FINGERLING NEW POTATOES, SKINS ON

1 TABLESPOON UNSALTED BUTTER

1 TABLESPOON COARSE SEA SALT

1/4 TEASPOON FRESHLY GROUND WHITE PEPPER

1/2 TABLESPOON CHOPPED PARSLEY, FOR GARNISH

1. Bring a medium saucepan of salted water to a boil over medium-high heat. Add the potatoes and parboil for 15 minutes, or until a fork pierces them easily. Drain in a colander.
2. Peel the skin off the potatoes while still hot, and then place them in a large mixing bowl with the butter. Season with the salt and pepper, toss well, garnish with the chopped parsley, and serve.

Pears Poached in Red Wine with Pistachio Ice Cream

Now this is a sexy dessert! Starting with the pears' undulating shapes and the deep maroon color of the sauce, this dish is as stunning to behold as it is good to eat. It's best when prepared the night before and stored in a jar in the fridge. That way the pears absorb the red wine and get a full dose of its color and flavor. The pears should be ripe but slightly firm, not too soft. As an alternative to the pistachio ice cream, serve with Chocolate Pot de Crème (page 165) or vanilla ice cream.

4 LARGE RIPE BOSC OR BARTLETT PEARS, SKINNED

1 (750-MILLILITER) BOTTLE RED WINE
(CABERNET SAUVIGNON, MERLOT,
OR OTHER FRUITY FULL-BODIED RED)

1 CUP PORT

1 CUP SUGAR

2 STRIPS OF LEMON ZEST

2 STRIPS OF ORANGE ZEST

2 CLOVES

2 CARDAMOM PODS

1 CINNAMON STICK

1/2 TABLESPOON WHOLE BLACK PEPPERCORNS

2 SLICES PEELED FRESH GINGER

1 PINT PISTACHIO ICE CREAM

1. Place all the ingredients except the ice cream in a deep pot, making sure the pears are fully submerged in the liquid. Bring to a boil over high heat, reduce the heat to medium-low, and simmer until the pears are just tender but not soft, 30 minutes. Test the pears for doneness by carefully piercing them with a paring knife: They should be soft and tender, and the knife should slip in and out without pulling apart the fruit.
2. Remove the pot from the stove and allow the pears to cool in their liquid. Once cool, cover the pot and place it in the refrigerator for at least 2 hours. (Alternatively, transfer the pears to a bowl or jar, cover, and refrigerate overnight.)
3. To serve, remove the pears from the pot with a slotted spoon, and allow them to drain upright on paper towels. Place them in small serving bowls, divide the liquid equally among the bowls, and serve with pistachio ice cream.

Shortbread Cookies

Makes 12 cookies

4 ounces unsalted butter,
softened at room temperature for 1 hour
½ cup confectioners' sugar
1 large egg
1 teaspoon vanilla powder
(or 2 drops vanilla extract, but the powder
is much preferable)
Pinch of salt
1 ⅓ cups sifted all-purpose flour
Granulated sugar, for sprinkling

1. In a large bowl, beat the butter and confectioners' sugar together until creamy. Add the egg, vanilla, salt, and flour. Mix together with a wooden spoon or your hand until it forms a dough. Don't overmix. Wrap the dough in plastic wrap and place it in the refrigerator for 1 hour.
2. Preheat the oven to 350°F.
3. Roll the dough out to a thickness of ¼ inch. Cut it into 2 × 3-inch rectangles. Or use a cookie cutter to make some other shapes. Pierce the pieces of dough with a fork three to five times each.
4. Line a baking sheet with parchment paper. Place the pieces of dough, evenly spaced, on the parchment-covered sheet. Bake for 15 minutes, or until lightly brown on top. Allow to cool, sprinkle with granulated sugar, and serve.

NOTE The cookies can be stored in a covered airtight container for up to 1 week.

Edited Elegance

for 6

This is an extremely elegant setting, but the meal is really quite informal and features a down-to-earth menu of French country food. The dinner is staged at an exquisitely appointed apartment overlooking Manhattan's Central Park. Its owners, my good friends Lars and Elizabeth Enochson, commissioned my close friend Charles Allem to complete the interior, and together they did a spectacular job. Many of the furniture pieces, along with the paneling, were created by Viscount Linley. The design and decor radiate an atmosphere of restrained elegance, so I set out to put together a dinner party in that same spirit. If you keep all the elements simple, casual, and relaxed, it's hard for everyone not to look and feel cool and comfortable.

I love collecting beautiful things, and some of them are quite valuable. Yet I also never shy away from combining them with ordinary, everyday items as long as the look is right. I have absolutely no problem mixing Baccarat stemware with colored water glasses ordered from a mail-order catalog or found at a flea market. It's not about the labeling, it's about the look.

And you shouldn't leave your collectibles locked up or stashed away. Use them, mix them up with inexpensive items, don't get hung up on formality. The most important thing is that your collectibles see the daylight—or the night life. No matter how formal the setting and the accoutrements, the feeling of the evening can still be casual and relaxed.

The centerpiece is a decorative urn filled with gorgeous big succulent grapes. The red color of the grapes is reflected in the napkins and picked up again in the rim of the glasses and in the plates. Amid all this well-calculated, manufactured splendor, the moss provides an element of unadorned natural beauty.

In keeping with its French country theme, the meal is served family style from platters. There's always a moment for a bit of theatricality in every meal. On this occasion, I accentuate the presentation of the salad by first passing around the big communal bowl so everyone can help themselves. Then I circle the table and, with a flourish, carefully deposit one poached egg on top of each guest's mound of greens.

The Cocktail Hour (or Less)

When I invite guests for eight o'clock, I want to be sure that everyone's seated at the table by nine. Cocktails should never last longer than an hour or even forty-five minutes on a weeknight. Otherwise the party may drag on. In today's fast-paced world, it's far better to spend two hours of quality time with friends than to subject everyone to three or four hours of eating and drinking to the point where they glance at their watches and notice it's eleven-thirty with no sign of dessert in sight. I like to approach every dinner with my friends like a theater performance: a carefully thought-out story with beginning, middle, and end. There's a sense of rhythm, which keeps up the momentum. Before anybody so much as thinks of checking their watches, the next activity is already taking place. As a host, you want to keep things moving, but never hurried. So you can also sit back, relax, and enjoy the time spent with your friends!

The Menu: Supper for Six

APPETIZER
FRISÉE WITH CROUTONS AND CRISPY BACON

MAIN COURSE
BRAISED SHORT RIBS
MEDLEY OF VEGETABLES
MASHED POTATOES WITH CELERY ROOT
MOUSSELINE

DESSERT
BERRY CLAFOUTIS WITH VANILLA ICE CREAM

TO DRINK
COCKTAIL DE NUIT: COURVOISIERPOLITAN
(OR CV COSMO, FOR SHORT)

WINE: HEARTY RED
A CLASSIC BORDEAUX-STYLE BLEND, INCLUDING CABERNET SAUVIGNON, MERLOT, AND CABERNET FRANC, HAS THE COMBINATION OF POWERFUL FLAVORS AND SUBTLE NUANCES TO BLEND EFFORTLESSLY WITH THE SHORT RIBS AS THEY MELT IN YOUR MOUTH. TRY THE LANCASTER RESERVE FROM CALIFORNIA'S ALEXANDER VALLEY IN SONOMA COUNTY OR SOME EQUIVALENT.

TIMING As soon as you get home—even before you walk the dog—start preparing the main dish, which requires long, slow cooking in the oven. While it quietly bubbles away, filling the house with mouthwatering aromas, you can happily go about your other business. Everything else can be prepped in advance. The vegetables can be sautéed together at the last minute. The dessert, which takes a little over an hour to bake, can go into the oven during cocktail hour, to be ready at the end of dinner.

COURVOISIERPOLITAN

In the mid to late 1990s, the Cosmopolitan became the drink of choice among hip, savvy urbanites—or anyone who aspired to that status. Here's a variation on the Cosmo with Courvoisier instead of the usual vodka—call it a Courvoisierpolitan, or CV Cosmo, for short.

4 OUNCES COURVOISIER
4 OUNCES TRIPLE SEC
4 OUNCES CRANBERRY JUICE
6 OUNCES LIME JUICE
SLICES OF ORANGE PEEL, FOR GARNISH

1. Chill 6 martini glasses (see below).
2. Pour all the liquid ingredients in a shaker filled with ice. Shake vigorously, then strain into the glasses. Garnish each with a slice of orange peel.

411: Chilling a Martini Glass

The best way to chill your martini glasses is to fill them with ice, top off with cold water, and let them sit for at least 10 minutes. Once you've shaken the cocktail, quickly empty the ice water from each glass and strain the mixture into it. This is an extra step, but it's well worth it in my estimation. Any "martini type" of cocktail—served straight up, without the cooling benefit of ice—is better when served very cold, and it stays much colder if served in a chilled glass. You could also simply place the empty glasses in your freezer (or refrigerator) about an hour in advance.

OTT

Use a small implement called a pithier, which has several slicing holes at its end, to cut thin curlicues of orange peel for the garnish. It's an elegant touch.

Frisée with Croutons and Crispy Bacon

This is a classic French *salade aux lardons*—thick-cut bacon, croutons, and poached egg. Since the frisée is a relatively delicate and airy lettuce, vegetable oil is used instead of olive oil, which might prove too heavy. The vinaigrette can be made in advance and kept in a glass jar in the refrigerator for up to 1 week. Use it on any type of salad or greens.

1/2 POUND SLAB BACON
(OR PANCETTA), CUT INTO 1/4-INCH CUBES

3 TABLESPOONS SHERRY VINEGAR

2 TEASPOONS DIJON MUSTARD

1 GARLIC CLOVE, CRUSHED

1 TEASPOON COARSE SEA SALT

1/2 TEASPOON FRESHLY GROUND BLACK PEPPER

1/3 CUP VEGETABLE OIL

1 TEASPOON WHITE VINEGAR

6 EGGS, POACHED FOR 2 TO 3 MINUTES EACH
(SEE NOTE)

1 1/2 POUNDS CHICORY OR BABY FRISÉE
(3 HEADS), WASHED, BROKEN INTO SMALL PIECES, AND DRIED

CROUTONS (RECIPE FOLLOWS)

1 TABLESPOON CHOPPED FRESH FLAT-LEAF PARSLEY

1. Bring a medium pot of water to a boil and blanch the bacon in it for 2 minutes to remove the excess fat. Drain in a colander.

2. Place the bacon in a small pan over medium heat and fry it until crispy, 3 to 5 minutes. Remove from the pan and drain on paper towels.

3. Prepare the vinaigrette by combining the sherry vinegar, mustard, garlic, salt, and pepper in a mixing bowl with a wire whisk. Continue whisking vigorously while slowly adding the vegetable oil.

4. Fill a shallow saucepan with enough water to submerge the eggs, add the white vinegar (never any salt), place over medium heat, and bring to a simmer (not a rolling boil). Crack the eggs carefully, just above the water, and let them slide into the water so they don't break up. (Alternatively, crack them into a small cup or bowl and carefully pour them into the water.) Poach the eggs in batches of two for 2 to 3 minutes apiece. Using a slotted spoon, transfer the poached eggs to a plate covered with paper towels to drain. Serve while still warm.

5. Toss the salad in a bowl with the vinaigrette, add half the bacon, and add the croutons. Season with salt and pepper and toss well. Place the salad on individual plates and lay a poached egg on each. Sprinkle with the remainder of the bacon and the parsley.

NOTE If you choose to poach the eggs in advance, they can be stored in a bowl of ice-cold water in the refrigerator for the day. To reheat, drain the water, cover the bowl with plastic wrap, and heat in the microwave on the high setting for 30 seconds to 1 minute.

Soft-boiled eggs can be substituted for poached eggs in this recipe. To soft-boil an egg, plunge it into a saucepan of salted boiling water for 7 minutes. To prevent eggs from cracking during boiling, be sure there are no hairline cracks in the eggs when raw, and add about 2 tablespoons of salt per quart of water. Remove the eggs from the water and peel under a stream of cold water. Once peeled, slice the eggs and fold them into the salad.

CROUTONS

1/2 LOAF OF CRUSTY BREAD, CUT INTO 1/2-INCH CUBES

1 TABLESPOON OLIVE OIL

1 TABLESPOON GRATED PARMESAN CHEESE

1/2 TEASPOON SALT

1/8 TEASPOON FRESHLY GROUND BLACK PEPPER

1. Preheat the oven to 400°F.

2. Combine the bread, olive oil, Parmesan, and salt and pepper in a large bowl, and toss well.

3. Transfer the bread cubes to a baking sheet and bake for 3 to 5 minutes, until golden brown.

BRAISED SHORT RIBS

While this recipe does take some time to cook, the actual preparation is simple, straightforward, and quick (about 20 minutes), and the rewards are tremendous. There is nothing quite as tender, juicy, and heart-warming as a hearty braised meat dish like this one. The pot liquor makes a rich, savory sauce. Since it's cooked for close to 2 hours, the juices will concentrate very nicely, especially with the addition of the tomato paste. If you like your gravy a little thicker, dredge the meat in flour, then pat it dry before browning it. Just that residue of flour in the pot will make a difference over the long, slow cooking period.

12 TO 18 SHORT RIBS OF BEEF
(APPROXIMATELY 1 1/2 INCHES THICK BY 3 TO 4 INCHES LONG)

1 TABLESPOON COARSE SEA SALT

1 TABLESPOON FRESHLY GROUND BLACK PEPPER

2 TABLESPOONS VEGETABLE OIL

2 MEDIUM YELLOW ONIONS,
PEELED AND CUT INTO 8 PIECES

3 CELERY STALKS,
CLEANED AND CUT INTO 1/2-INCH PIECES

2 LARGE CARROTS,
CLEANED AND CUT INTO 1-INCH PIECES

1 WHOLE GARLIC HEAD, SKIN ON AND HALVED

3 TABLESPOONS TOMATO PASTE

1 (750-MILLILITER) BOTTLE FULL-BODIED RED WINE
(MERLOT, CABERNET SAUVIGNON, OR SOME EQUIVALENT)

1 1/2 CUPS VEAL STOCK,
PLUS MORE AS NEEDED (RECIPE FOLLOWS)

1 BOUQUET GARNI (SEE NOTE, PAGE 120)

1 TEASPOON COARSE SEA SALT

1/2 TEASPOON FRESHLY GROUND BLACK PEPPER

1 BATCH OF SAUTÉED MUSHROOMS (RECIPE FOLLOWS)

2 TABLESPOONS CHOPPED PARSLEY, FOR GARNISH

1. Preheat the oven to 350°F.

2. Season the ribs generously with salt and pepper. Place the vegetable oil in a roasting pan or heavy-bottomed pot large enough to hold all the ribs over medium-high heat. When the oil becomes smoky hot, place the ribs in the pot in a single layer and brown well on all four sides, approximately 5 minutes per side. If necessary, brown in batches; set aside each cooked batch and repeat until all ribs are browned.

3. Skim the excess fat from the pot using a large, flat spoon or ladle, lower the heat to medium, and then add the onions, celery, carrots, and garlic. Cook the vegetables until golden brown,

5 to 8 minutes. Deglaze the pot to remove any burned bits. Add the tomato paste, stir well, and continue cooking for 2 to 3 minutes. Add the red wine, reduce the heat to low, and scrape up any brown bits with a wooden spoon.

4. Return the ribs to the pot. Add just enough of the veal stock to cover the ribs. Add the bouquet garni, the 1 teaspoon coarse salt, and the 1/2 teaspoon freshly ground black pepper. Bring to a boil and cover. Place the pot in the oven and braise for 1 hour and 45 minutes to 2 hours, or until the meat is tender. Turn the ribs after 45 minutes. If the liquid starts to dry up, add more stock as needed. (Alternatively, the roast can be cooked on top of the stove over low heat.)

5. Remove the ribs from the pot and strain the remaining liquid through a fine sieve. Discard the vegetables. Return the liquid to the pot and bring to a boil over medium-high heat. Reduce for 5 to 10 minutes, or until thickened to a sauce-like consistency. Skim the fat with a large, flat spoon or ladle, and place the ribs in the pot. Add the sautéed mushrooms and mix well.

6. Transfer the ribs and sauce to a large platter, sprinkle with parsley, and serve.

411: Deglazing

Deglazing is a wonderful technique for making a quick sauce by capturing the delicious caramelized bits of food—usually meat—and cooking juices in a pan or skillet after sautéing, pan-frying, or roasting. Simply remove the main ingredient(s) from the pan, skim off the excess grease with a large spoon or ladle, add 3 to 4 tablespoons of liquid such as wine or stock (or water, in a pinch), leave the heat on medium, and scrape and stir the contents of the pan with a wooden spoon. Once the liquid has taken on a deep color, you've got a very basic sauce. If you like, go one step further by adding a cup or two more stock and/or reducing the sauce by boiling it until it reaches the thickness you desire. To finish it off, you might also choose to stir in some butter or cream, a vegetable purée, herbs, or other seasonings. But don't make a sauce this way if the pan residue is blackened or burned; it will turn out bitter.

SAUTÉED MUSHROOMS

1 TABLESPOON UNSALTED BUTTER

1 TABLESPOON OLIVE OIL

½ POUND WHITE BUTTON OR CREMINI MUSHROOMS,
CLEANED AND QUARTERED

SALT AND FRESHLY GROUND BLACK PEPPER, TO TASTE

Melt the butter with the oil in a small skillet over medium-high heat. Add the mushrooms, salt, and pepper. Sauté for 5 minutes, or until all the liquid has evaporated.

911

As a shortcut, simply add the quartered mushrooms to the pot juices in the last 5 minutes of reducing the sauce.

VEAL STOCK

6 POUNDS VEAL BONES

1 POUND ONIONS, COARSELY CHOPPED

1 POUND CARROTS, COARSELY CHOPPED

1 POUND CELERY, COARSELY CHOPPED

1 POUND LEEKS,
WASHED AND CUT INTO 2-INCH SECTIONS

1. Preheat the oven to 450°F. Roast the veal bones for 15 to 20 minutes, until they are dark brown.

2. Place the roasted bones and all the remaining ingredients in a large stockpot. Add enough cold water to cover the ingredients. Bring the water in the pot to a boil, reduce the heat to low, and simmer for 6 hours, skimming periodically to remove any grease.

3. Strain the stock and discard the solids. If you want to thicken the stock, clean the pot, return the stock to the pot, and boil it until it is reduced by up to 50 percent.

MASHED POTATOES WITH CELERY ROOT MOUSSELINE

Mousseline is a term usually used for mousse-like preparations that include whipped cream and/or egg whites to give them a lighter quality. I think you'll find this potato–celery root combo shares some of that fluffy texture.

2 LARGE CELERY ROOTS

JUICE OF 1 LEMON

4 LARGE YUKON GOLD POTATOES,
PEELED AND QUARTERED

1 TABLESPOON COARSE SEA SALT

1/4 CUP WHOLE MILK

2 TABLESPOONS UNSALTED BUTTER

1/2 TEASPOON SALT

1/4 TEASPOON WHITE PEPPER

MEDLEY OF VEGETABLES

Baby vegetables have become all the rage in America's best gourmet food shops over the past decade. They are chic and slightly exotic, and they possess a wonderful natural sweetness. They add an instant touch of elegance to any presentation; and, for convenience, they also cook quickly.

12 BABY TURNIPS, PEELED AND CLEANED
(IF ONLY LARGE TURNIPS ARE AVAILABLE,
PEEL AND CUT INTO 8 PIECES)

1/2 POUND GREEN BEANS, WASHED

1/2 POUND SUGAR SNAP PEAS, WASHED

12 BABY CARROTS, PEELED AND WASHED

1/2 POUND BABY YELLOW SQUASH
(IF ONLY LARGE SQUASH IS AVAILABLE, CUT INTO 2-INCH PIECES)

1 TABLESPOON UNSALTED BUTTER

1 TABLESPOON OLIVE OIL

1. Bring a large pot of salted water to a boil over medium-high heat. Add the turnips and cook for 5 minutes. Add the beans, peas, carrots, and squash and cook for an additional 3 to 5 minutes, or until al dente. Drain well in a colander. (The recipe can be prepared up to this point in advance; once they're cooked, place the vegetables in a bowl of ice-cold water and store in the fridge until ready to reheat.)

2. Return the vegetables to the pot. Add the butter and oil and sauté over medium heat until well warmed, 3 to 4 minutes. Transfer to a large platter and serve.

1. Peel the celery root, cut it into 1-inch cubes, and toss it in a bowl with the lemon juice. (This is to avoid discoloration, which comes from contact with the air. It is also cut much smaller than the potato since it's denser yet needs to cook at the same rate as the potato.)

2. Place the celery root and potato in a large pot, cover with water, add the coarse salt, and bring to a boil over high heat. Reduce the heat to medium-high and cook for 30 to 40 minutes, until the vegetables are tender—that is, when a knife tip will penetrate the celery root easily.

3. Drain the vegetables in a colander. Allow them to stand until all the liquid drains away so the potatoes don't become soggy. Pass through a food mill or a ricer into a mixing bowl while still hot.

4. While the vegetables are draining, place the milk and butter in a small saucepan over high heat and bring to a boil. Remove from the heat immediately, and combine with the potatoes and celery root. Whip the entire mixture with a wooden spoon until it is smooth and forms peaks. Adjust the consistency as desired by adding a little extra milk. Season with the salt and pepper.

Berry Clafoutis

Clafoutis is the French version of what is known as a cobbler in the United States. It comes from the French heartland—specifically the plateaus of the Limousin region, about three hundred miles south of Paris, where the countryside is rich in livestock, fruits, and game. The classic clafoutis was made from unpitted black cherries, but variations are made with many other fruits.

APPROXIMATELY ¼ CUP (4 TABLESPOONS)
UNSALTED BUTTER, FOR GREASING THE PAN,
PLUS 2 TABLESPOONS

¾ CUP SUGAR

1 ½ POUNDS MIXED BERRIES
(SUCH AS BLUEBERRIES, RASPBERRIES, BLACKBERRIES,
BOYSENBERRIES, OR QUARTERED STRAWBERRIES)
OR BLACK CHERRIES, PITTED (SEE NOTE)

4 LARGE EGGS

½ CUP ALL-PURPOSE FLOUR, SIFTED

4 TABLESPOONS RUM

1 ½ CUPS HEAVY WHIPPING CREAM

PINCH OF SALT

JUICE OF 1 LEMON

1. Preheat the oven to 350°F.

2. Grease a 2-quart ovenproof glass dish (8 × 8 × 2½ inches) with the butter and dust thoroughly with ¼ cup of the sugar: Place the sugar in the dish, shake the dish to distribute the sugar evenly, and discard the excess. Fill the dish with the fruit.

3. To make the batter: In a large mixing bowl, beat the eggs with the remaining ½ cup of sugar until smooth, about 1 minute. (This can be done by hand or with a mixer.) Add the sifted flour and mix until smooth. Melt the remaining 2 tablespoons of butter in a small saucepan over medium heat. Add the melted butter and rum to the batter, and mix until smooth. Add the heavy cream, salt, and lemon juice, and mix again until smooth. (If the mixture has lumps, pass through a fine strainer or chinois.)

4. Pour the batter on top of the fruit in the baking dish, making sure it is evenly distributed. Bake for 50 minutes, until the custard is set and the batter is golden brown on top. Serve warm with vanilla ice cream or whipped cream.

NOTE Store-bought berries have already been picked through to remove any clumps of dirt or other impurities. There is no need to wash them and risk turning them soggy with excess water. The only berries that need washing are strawberries, which are grown in sandy soil and will drain easily in a colander or when patted dry.

DIRTY MOVIES
FOR 6

At home in my New York City apartment, the room that serves as my office doubles as a cozy den and entertainment center. This particular dinner was a welcome interlude in the middle of a busy work week. (The formula also works well for a casual get-together on a quiet Sunday evening.) At the end of the business day, I gather up all my papers and put them away, and make a few basic preparations. Within minutes, I'm ready for guests to arrive and cocktails to be served.

I set up a bar in the corner of the room with a bottle each of red and white wine along with chilled bottles of water (flat and sparkling). Before we start the movie, everything's in place so nobody misses a frame. Guests are encouraged to help themselves at any time from the bar, which is right near the television and in full view of the screen.

I arranged place settings on the coffee table in front of the sofa. The color theme was black-on-black—appropriate for this rather sleek, urbane, sophisticated version of the proverbial TV dinner. There was a black rattan runner down the length of the table, black plates, black napkins, black flatware, and a black candle in front of each setting. Each place was provided with its own TV tray so our guests could eat at their seats while enjoying the show. Years ago, I found these marvelous Fornacetti trays, which are both beautiful and functional; they became the basis for a chic entertaining format. Anytime I see such a serving piece, I immediately ask myself, "How can I use that?" And the wheels begin to turn. . . .

The meal itself was the embodiment of simplicity. It's the ideal "bachelor dinner," and you don't have to be an accomplished chef to pull it off—far from it. It's also yet another illustration of the principle that if you choose the finest, freshest ingredients and prepare them simply without fuss you're virtually guaranteed success.

For the main course, the steaks and their two vegetable side dishes were lined up side by side and served on the same large tray. I presented both the appetizer course and the dessert in glasses, which made them easy to manipulate. The crab cocktail was in a pedestal coupe, the berries and sorbet in a rocks glass. Should anyone want to sit back and enjoy them, it'd be easy.

The Menu: Supper for Six

Appetizer
Crab Cocktail Salad

Main Course
Pan-Seared Aged New York Steak
Roasted Asparagus
Roasted Tomatoes

Dessert
Mixed Berry Salad with Scotch and Sorbet
Orange Tuiles

To Drink
Cocktail de Nuit: Watermelon Martini
Wine: A full-bodied Red
Cabernet Sauvignon, a Rioja or Ribera del Duero from Spain,
or a Barolo from northern Italy

TIMING Have the watermelon purée ready and shake the 'tinis when the guests first arrive. The dessert needs to chill for an hour in the fridge, so make it in advance; if you're going to bake the cookies at home, they need to be done in advance as well. The tomatoes take 15 to 20 minutes to roast, as does the asparagus, and the steaks take 12 to 14 minutes with a short resting period; so start these items in that order. I suggest presenting the appetizer course while the tomatoes are roasting; then take a break to cook the steak and asparagus; then start the movie as dessert is served or after the meal is finished. As an alternative, the steak can be seared in advance, then finished in the oven during a short break in the movie. Or prepare the tomatoes and asparagus, then place them in the oven while cooking the steak. If the movie's on television, do all this before it starts. If it's on video or DVD, you can pause or stop whenever you wish.

When you're watching TV, you don't want to have to deal with a bowl; you can hold the glass in your hand, bring it up to your mouth very easily without feeling ill-mannered, and still concentrate on the movie.

The menu—a cold seafood-salad appetizer preceding a good old-fashioned steak—is an American standby. It's the kind of meal you would have ordered in the forties, fifties, or sixties at the "21" Club in New York or Chasen's in L.A., which I think makes it particularly appropriate movie fare. The main concession we're making to modernity is avoiding potatoes or other heavy starches in favor of two healthy vegetables. Also, if the food is too heavy, you'll fall asleep halfway through the movie—and we don't want that!

For dessert service, I used oval rocks glasses with square black plates for the berries and sorbet. After the dinner was cleared away, we brought in a hot, fresh bowl of popcorn and settled in to watch the rest of our James Bond movie.

Watermelon Martini

To make a delightful juice or cocktail ingredient, all you have to do is pulse some watermelon—preferably seedless, either red or yellow—in a blender. It's mostly water anyway, and it has lovely color and a subtle, light flavor.

¼ LARGE SEEDLESS WATERMELON

12 OUNCES VODKA

JUICE OF 1 LIME

SPLASH OF SIMPLE SYRUP (SEE PAGE 47)

6 WATERMELON BALLS,
SCOOPED OUT WITH A MELON-BALLER, FOR GARNISH

1 LIME, THINLY SLICED, FOR GARNISH

1. Chill 6 martini glasses (see page 181).
2. Pulse the watermelon in a blender to create a purée (you should have about 1½ cups). Pour the vodka, lime juice, and simple syrup into a shaker filled with ice. Shake vigorously, then strain into the chilled glasses. Garnish with a watermelon ball on the rim of the glass and float a slice of lime in the center.

Crab Cocktail Salad

This is a classic appetizer that's all about presentation—not preparation—which is why I like to serve it in some type of vessel that makes a statement: a cocktail glass, a champagne coup, or a decorative cup. It should always be made from fresh crabmeat. If you want to add more volume to this salad, use the iceberg lettuce to make cups for the crab mixture, and place the whole assembly on a bed of baby arugula or other greens.

¾ CUP KETCHUP

½ CUP PREPARED HORSERADISH

JUICE OF 1 LEMON

½ TEASPOON TABASCO SAUCE

1½ POUNDS LUMP CRABMEAT,
PICKED OVER TO ELIMINATE STRAY PIECES OF BONE OR SHELL

1 HEAD OF ICEBERG LETTUCE, WASHED AND SHREDDED

¼ TEASPOON CAYENNE PEPPER

1 LEMON, CUT INTO 6 WEDGES

1. In a large bowl, combine the ketchup, horseradish, lemon juice, and Tabasco and mix well. (This mixture can be prepared in advance and stored in the fridge until you are ready to assemble the dish.)
2. Gently fold the crab into the seasoned mayonnaise. Divide the lettuce among 6 bowls or glasses, and spoon the crab mixture over each. Garnish each with a dash of cayenne pepper and serve with lemon wedges.

PAN-SEARED AGED NEW YORK STEAK

411: Steaks Done to Order at Your Fingertips

To gauge the doneness of a steak, give it a poke with your index finger. Now compare the firmness of the meat to the flesh at the base of your thumb while pressing the tip of your thumb to a finger: With the thumb pressing the index finger, it's soft with a lot of give—that's rare. With the tip of the thumb against the middle finger, you begin to feel some springiness—that's medium rare. Thumb to ring finger is medium; and thumb to pinkie is firm and well done.

The finest butchers, meat purveyors, and dining establishments still take the time to dry-age a select few of their finest cuts of steak. This involves storing them, unwrapped to afford air exposure, for up to six weeks at a temperature between 32° and 36°F. Naturally occurring enzymes within the meat begin the process of protein breakdown, which tenderizes the meat. It also dries out, losing up to 20 percent of its weight through evaporation, which concentrates its flavors. What you get is a tastier, more tender cut. It also costs more. In my estimation, it's well worth it.

The cut I'm calling for here is a boneless top loin, which is generally known as a New York steak, New York strip steak, or just strip steak. In a porterhouse or T-bone, there are two sections, one on each side of the bone; this New York cut is the same as the larger section of the porterhouse, with the bone removed. (The smaller section is the filet mignon.) A rib-eye would be a good substitute for the strip. Just be sure you get a well-marbled "prime" or at the very least "choice" cut, and preferably a dry-aged one.

4 AGED NEW YORK STRIP STEAKS,
CUT 1 ½ TO 2 INCHES THICK, AT ROOM TEMPERATURE (SEE NOTE)
4 TABLESPOONS COARSE SEA SALT
3 TABLESPOONS COARSELY CRACKED BLACK PEPPER
¼ CUP VEGETABLE OIL

1. Season the steaks generously with salt and pepper.
2. Heat the oil in a heavy-bottomed pan over high heat. When the oil is very hot but not yet smoking, cook the steaks on one side for 4 minutes. Turn the steaks over and cook for another 4 minutes. Cook each side again for 2 minutes and then each end for a minute. Allow to rest for about 5 minutes before slicing and serving. (Adjust the cooking time according to thickness of steaks and desired doneness; for example, thinner steaks might take just 3 minutes per side before flipping. The extra flipping helps ensure a well-cooked, nicely caramelized exterior with plenty of delicious juices running inside.)

NOTE A steak should always be at room temperature before you cook it, so if it is refrigerated take it out at least an hour in advance. If it's cold, right out of the fridge, you're going to get a steak that's seared on the outside and nearly raw on the inside. When it's cooked at room temperature, you'll see a nice gradation of doneness from the crispy, caramelized exterior to the pink and red center. In addition, a cold steak will take longer to cook, invalidating most recipe cooking times.

911

Pressed for time? "Roast" the asparagus in the microwave. Simply place all the ingredients in a microwave-safe dish, add 2 or 3 tablespoons of water, cover with microwave-safe plastic wrap, and cook on the high setting for 8 to 10 minutes.

OTT: Steak Presentation

Cover an entire wood cutting board with a layer of rosemary, place the done steak on top, and serve. It's guaranteed to leave a lasting impression.

You might like to garnish your steak with crispy fried sage (see Pan-Roasted Loin of Veal, pages 17–18).

Roasted Asparagus

Unless the asparagus is young, thin, and tender, you'll want to peel it with a vegetable peeler (see page 66).

3 BUNCHES OF THICK ASPARAGUS
(4 SPEARS PER PERSON), PEELED

1/4 CUP OLIVE OIL

1 TEASPOON COARSE SEA SALT, PLUS MORE TO TASTE

1/2 TEASPOON FRESHLY GROUND BLACK PEPPER,
PLUS MORE TO TASTE

1. Preheat the oven to 350°F.
2. Lay the asparagus in a single layer on a baking sheet. Drizzle with olive oil and season with the salt and pepper. Place in he oven for 15 minutes, or until the asparagus is al dente (still slightly chewy) and brownish on top.
3. Transfer to a platter and serve.

Roasted Tomatoes

1/4 CUP CHOPPED FRESH FLAT-LEAF PARSLEY

1 GARLIC CLOVE, MINCED (ABOUT 1 TEASPOON)

1/4 CUP BREAD CRUMBS

1/3 CUP GRATED PARMIGIANO-REGGIANO

1/4 CUP OLIVE OIL

1 TEASPOON SALT

1/2 TEASPOON FRESHLY GROUND BLACK PEPPER

6 LARGE RIPE TOMATOES, SKIN ON, TOPS CUT OFF

1. Preheat the oven to 350°F.
2. In a medium bowl, combine the parsley, garlic, bread crumbs, cheese, and olive oil; mix well. Season the tomatoes with salt and pepper, and spread an equal portion of the bread-crumb mixture on the cut side of each.
3. Place the tomatoes in a baking pan and bake for 15 to 20 minutes, until they are tender and the topping is browned.

Mixed Berry Salad with Scotch and Sorbet

Here's a light, healthy, refreshing dessert that takes just a few minutes to pull together and an hour or more to chill. You can add ½ cup of mango purée or ripe mango pulp to the fruit mixture. The dish also works well with strawberry, lemon, mango, or lime sorbet.

½ CUP GREEN SEEDLESS GRAPES
½ CUP RED SEEDLESS GRAPES
½ CUP MELON BALLS (SEE NOTE)
½ CUP MIXED BERRIES IN SEASON
⅓ CUP SCOTCH WHISKEY
2 TABLESPOONS SUGAR
1 PINT RASPBERRY SORBET

1. In a medium bowl, combine all the ingredients except the sorbet. Refrigerate for 1 hour.
2. Distribute the fruit evenly among 6 rocks glasses, making sure to use all the syrup. Top each glass with a scoop of the sorbet.

NOTE You can buy a small utensil called a melon-baller and scoop the melon balls out of fresh melons for yourself. One half cup of melon balls, taken from a full-size cantaloupe or honeydew, will be the equivalent of one medium wedge.

Orange Tuiles

A tuile is a delicious, delicate thin, round cookie. Making these cookies as opposed to buying them is strictly optional—for the home chef who's not pressed for time. Store-bought equivalents abound. If you do choose to make them, do it in advance, and double the recipe if you like. They make great snacks and accompaniments for other desserts. Store them in an airtight container for one or two days.

MAKES 1 DOZEN

2 TABLESPOONS UNSALTED BUTTER
¾ CUP CONFECTIONERS' SUGAR
¼ CUP ALL-PURPOSE FLOUR
½ CUP BLANCHED ALMONDS, COARSELY CHOPPED
ZEST OF ½ ORANGE, GRATED
2 TABLESPOONS FRESH ORANGE JUICE

1. Preheat the oven to 350°F.
2. Melt the butter in a small saucepan over medium heat, then transfer to a glass bowl and allow to cool to room temperature.
3. In a medium bowl, combine the sugar, flour, almonds, and orange zest. Using a wooden spoon, stir in the melted butter. Add the orange juice and stir until the batter is smooth. Cover the bowl and place it in the refrigerator for 1 hour.
4. Line a baking sheet with parchment paper. Spoon the batter, 1 teaspoonful at a time, into mounds on the baking sheet. Leave about 4 inches between the mounds for expansion when they bake. Bake for 5 minutes, or until golden brown or caramel-colored on top. (If still white, they are too soft.) Remove the baking sheet from the oven and allow the cookies to cool. Separate them from the parchment paper and serve.

SOCIAL LADDER
FOR 4

For this intimate get-together, I made use of a space that doubles as a drawing room and guest room in a spectacular pied-à-terre overlooking Manhattan's Central Park. The setting and the view of the sunset were simply breathtaking. Of course, not everyone's home has this vista. But many of us do have access to nice views from somewhere in our house. The point is that it doesn't have to be the dining room. Variety is the spice of life. Why eat in the same place every night? You can find a nook in the kitchen, living room, den, or on the patio, deck, balcony, or porch, and set up the area for dining.

I positioned the table right in the window to take advantage of the gorgeous view and sunset for an early dinner before we went to the theater. We had four great tickets to see an amazing show, so we didn't want to eat anything very heavy.

The decor of the room followed an edgy black-and-white scheme, so I decided to take that idea and run with it. I had a table-cloth in mind that had big, bold, black-and-white stripes. As I visualized matching china and flatware, I began to realize this was a real flashback to the early 1960s, so that's where I decided to go with the menu. Beginning with the Shrimp Avocado Ritz, followed by the stuffed cornish hens, and right through to the dessert, which features Bailey's Irish Cream liqueur, it's a meal that harks back to the glory days of that fabulous decade. It's the sort of menu that Jacqueline Kennedy would have served for a dinner in the White House at the height of Camelot.

Appetizer
Shrimp Avocado Ritz

Main Course
Stuffed Cornish Hens
Black-and-White Rice

Dessert
Bailey's Irish Cream Mousse

To Drink
Cocktails de Nuit: Black Russians
and White Russians

Wine: Pinot Noir
A deep, elegant Pinot Noir is the classic accompaniment for an earthy dish like the game hens. Both California and Oregon turn out some Pinots that are really special. Try the El Molino, from one of the oldest wineries in Napa Valley, or a suitable equivalent.

Advance Preparation Is Key

Just a bit of advance preparation takes ninety percent of the stress and strain out of home entertaining. For example, I always make sure that prior to the guests' arrival, the table is set, music is playing, the lights are dimmed, the candles are lit, and the drinks are ready (white wine, water, and soft drinks chilled; red wine opened; cocktail ingredients at hand and ready for mixing). Just these five deft touches instantly transform your home into a welcoming party zone. Furthermore, if you've got the dinner prepped and ready to go, you'll have the freedom to chat. Sometimes, if I have a party planned at the end of a busy day, I'll even set the table the night before. I know I'm getting home at seven, the dinner's at eight-thirty, I've got a little over an hour of cooking to do, and I don't want to be overburdened by having to set the table.

Don't Always Do It in the Dining Room

It's a good idea to arrange several different venues for entertaining within your home—kitchen, dining room, living room, breakfast room, television room, family room or den, patio, deck, or balcony. That way you have built-in variety and versatility. You make space for groups of different sizes, for different occasions, and for varying levels of formality.

TIMING The hens take 1 hour to roast and about 30 minutes of preparation; get them ready in advance and put them in the oven just before the guests arrive. The dessert needs to be chilled for 3 hours, so it should be made in advance—the night before or the morning of. Prepare the cocktail sauce in advance, if you like, and store it in the fridge like mayonnaise; the rest of the first course can be pulled together quickly, after you put the hens in the oven. Cook the two types of rice in advance, then mix and sauté to warm them just prior to serving.

BLACK RUSSIANS AND WHITE RUSSIANS

I couldn't think of a better cocktail—or, rather, pair of cocktails—to go with a black-and-white–themed dinner. The coffee and cream put you in a mellow, relaxed but alert mood, and of course the names of these drinks are magical and evocative.

BLACK RUSSIAN

8 OUNCES VODKA

6 OUNCES COFFEE LIQUEUR

Pour 2 ounces of vodka and 1½ ounces of coffee liqueur into each of 4 rocks glasses full of ice, stir, and serve.

WHITE RUSSIAN

8 OUNCES VODKA

6 OUNCES COFFEE LIQUEUR

4 TABLESPOONS HEAVY CREAM

Pour 2 ounces of vodka, 1½ ounces of coffee liqueur, and 1 tablespoon of cream into each of 4 rocks glasses full of ice, stir, and serve.

SHRIMP AVOCADO RITZ

How can you not love this combination of subtle flavors—the smooth, rich, green avocado and the equally rich, mildly piquant shrimp salad? It's amazing how far a simple concoction of shrimp, pink cocktail sauce, and lemon will take you. This is a classic recipe, created at the Hotel Ritz in Paris many years ago and now found in numerous variations throughout the world. Growing up, whenever we went out for a fancy meal or special occasion, it was *the* choice item on the menu as far as I was concerned.

2 LARGE EGG YOLKS

I TEASPOON DIJON MUSTARD

½ CUP VEGETABLE OIL

DASH OF TABASCO SAUCE

I TEASPOON BRANDY

2 TABLESPOONS KETCHUP

JUICE OF ½ LEMON

¼ TEASPOON SALT

⅛ TEASPOON FRESHLY GROUND BLACK PEPPER

I POUND COOKED SHRIMP (SEE NOTE), DEVEINED

2 LARGE AVOCADOS

I HEAD OF ICEBERG LETTUCE

4 GRAPEFRUIT SEGMENTS, MEMBRANES REMOVED

¼ TEASPOON PAPRIKA, FOR GARNISH

1. Prepare the cocktail sauce. Place the egg yolks and mustard in a mixing bowl and beat with a whisk. Gradually add the oil to the mixture, constantly whisking until it emulsifies to the consistency of mayonnaise. Add the Tabasco, brandy, ketchup, lemon juice, salt, and pepper, and mix well. (The sauce can be stored in a covered glass container in the refrigerator for up to a week.)
2. Cut the cooked and cleaned shrimp into 1-inch cubes. Combine it with the cocktail sauce in a large bowl and mix well.
3. Halve the avocados (see Note), remove the pits, but don't peel. Place equal amounts of the shrimp salad in the pit hollows of the avocado halves, filling them and creating mounds.
4. Arrange beds of iceberg lettuce leaves on salad plates and place a stuffed avocado half on each. Top with a segment of grapefruit, sprinkle with paprika, and serve.

NOTE This recipe calls for cooked shrimp. To poach your own, place enough salted water in a large saucepan to cover the shrimp by about ½ inch. Bring the water to a boil over high heat, and then reduce the heat to medium-low, add the shrimp, and simmer until the shrimp turn pink, 3 to 5 minutes. If you want to add a dash of flavor, you can poach the shrimp in a court-bouillon. Place water in a large sauté pan or skillet to a depth of 1 to 2 inches. Add ½ cup white wine, one large carrot cut into ¼-inch rounds, a rib of celery cut into ½-inch sections, a medium white onion sliced, 1 sprig of parsley, a tablespoon of white peppercorns, a bay leaf, and a sprig of thyme. Bring the water to a boil and simmer for 30 minutes. Then drop the shrimp in the court-bouillon to poach until pink, draining them and refreshing them in cold water before use.

NOTE If you're cutting the avocados in advance, rub the exposed surfaces with lemon juice to avoid discoloration.

911

Instead of making your own, buy a good prepared mayonnaise in the store; simply add the above-specified quantities of Tabasco, brandy, ketchup, mustard, and lemon juice to ⅔ cup mayonnaise, and proceed with the recipe.

STUFFED CORNISH HENS

Cornish hens, properly referred to as rock Cornish hens or rock Cornish game hens, are a hybrid of two breeds of small chicken. In this recipe, I call for four hens of about 1¼ pounds each, which make ideal individual servings. We're essentially treating the hens as miniature turkeys, stuffing and roasting them with periodic bastings. I created a moist, savory stuffing featuring nuts, bread, and sausage meat. You can use it to stuff pretty much any bird, including the Thanksgiving turkey. The big advantage over a turkey, of course, is that these little birds take only an hour to cook, not a whole day.

4 TABLESPOONS (¼ STICK) UNSALTED BUTTER

1 MEDIUM YELLOW ONION, DICED

⅛ POUND (2 STRIPS) DICED PANCETTA (OPTIONAL),
SLICED ¼ INCH THICK

½ POUND SWEET PORK SAUSAGE,
CASINGS REMOVED AND MEAT CRUMBLED

½ TABLESPOON CHOPPED FRESH THYME

1 TABLESPOON CHOPPED FRESH FLAT-LEAF PARSLEY

2 SLICES WHITE SANDWICH BREAD,
CUT INTO ¼-INCH CUBES AND LIGHTLY TOASTED

1 LARGE EGG

¼ CUP COARSELY CHOPPED TOASTED WALNUTS
(SEE NOTE)

¼ CUP COARSELY CHOPPED TOASTED PISTACHIOS

¼ CUP COARSELY CHOPPED TOASTED ALMONDS

¼ CUP COARSELY CHOPPED TOASTED HAZELNUTS

2 TO 3 CUPS CHICKEN STOCK (PAGE 120),
ENOUGH TO COVER THE BOTTOM OF THE ROASTING PANS
TO A DEPTH OF ½ INCH

1 TABLESPOON COARSE SEA SALT

½ TABLESPOON FRESHLY GROUND BLACK PEPPER

4 CORNISH HENS, ABOUT 1½ POUNDS EACH

1. Preheat the oven to 375°F.

2. Melt 2 tablespoons of the butter in a large sauté pan over medium heat. Add the onion and pancetta, and sauté for 4 minutes, until soft. Add the sausage meat and sauté, stirring, until brown, about 5 minutes. Remove the contents of the pan to a large mixing bowl and allow to cool. When cool, add the thyme and parsley and mix well. Add the toasted bread cubes, egg, nuts (see Note), and 2 tablespoons of the chicken stock. Mix well and season with salt and pepper.

3. Wash the Cornish hens in cold running water and pat dry with paper towels. Season the hens well inside and out with salt and pepper. Stuff the hens with 2 to 3 spoonfuls of stuffing each. Tie the legs together with kitchen string to cover the cavities so the stuffing will not spill out.

4. Melt the remaining 2 tablespoons of butter in the sauté pan. Place two of the hens in each of two ovenproof glass baking dishes. Brush the hens on the outside with the melted butter. Fill the baking dishes with chicken stock to a depth of ½ inch. Place the dishes in the oven and roast for 1 hour, basting three or four times. If the liquid begins to dry up, add more stock as needed. The hens are done when the juices run clear if you poke them near the thigh with a skewer.

5. Remove the pan from the oven, cut the string, and place the hens on serving plates. Skim the pan juices of any excess fat and use as a sauce (there's no need to reduce it). Serve the hens with Black-and-White Rice (recipe follows) on the side.

NOTE Measure all the nuts after you've chopped them, then toast them: Place the nuts in a skillet over medium heat or in the toaster oven, evenly distributed, for 3 to 5 minutes, until they have just turned a darker shade of color.

BLACK-AND-WHITE RICE

You could easily serve plain white rice and it would be incredibly tasty, soaking up the cooking juices from the roasted hens. But why not follow your color scheme to the max? With a little extra effort, you can have a lovely mix of black and white rices, which provides both color and texture contrasts. The wild rice also gives the meal a nice gamey flavor twist.

1 CUP WHITE RICE
1 CUP WILD RICE
1 TABLESPOON BUTTER

1. Cook the rices according to their respective package directions. (They cannot be cooked together, but they can be cooked in advance and set aside in a bowl.)
2. Melt the butter in a saucepan or skillet over medium-low heat, add the cooked rices, stir to combine, and sauté for 1 to 2 minutes (or until heated through if they've already cooled). Fluff the rice and serve on a platter alongside the Cornish hens.

BAILEY'S IRISH CREAM MOUSSE

I know the word *rich* is overused, but how could you not apply it to a dessert like this? It contains whole eggs, sugar, and cream with a healthy dollop of Bailey's Irish Cream. Chilled and served in martini glasses, it's an elegant, luscious retro finale for this scrumptious feast.

5 LARGE EGGS, SEPARATED
1 CUP BAILEY'S IRISH CREAM
1/4 OUNCE (1 PACKAGE) GELATIN POWDER
1 CUP HEAVY WHIPPING CREAM
3 OUNCES SUGAR
PINCH OF SALT
1/2 PINT CHOCOLATE SORBET
WHITE CHOCOLATE, FOR GARNISH

1. Fill a 1-quart saucepan about two-thirds full with water. Bring to a boil, then lower the heat to medium-low so the water is just simmering. Place a glass bowl on top of the saucepan so that the steam from the pan heats it, but the water doesn't touch the bottom of the bowl. Combine the egg yolks and the Bailey's in the bowl and beat until light and fluffy. (Do not overcook or you will make scrambled eggs.) Set aside.
2. Place the gelatin in a large mixing bowl, add 1/4 cup water, and stir to dissolve it. Add the egg yolk mixture and stir well. In another bowl, whip the cream and sugar together, then gently add them to the egg yolk mixture.
3. Place the egg whites in a large bowl with a pinch of salt and beat with a large whisk until they form soft peaks. (Alternatively, you can do this in an electric mixer with a whisk attachment.) Fold the egg whites into the egg-cream-sugar mixture, then divide the mousse evenly among 4 martini glasses or serving bowls. Refrigerate for at least 3 hours. Before serving, top with 1 scoop of chocolate sorbet and garnish with shaved white chocolate.

NOTE This recipe yields 6 servings, which means you'll have 2 left over for tomorrow—or for a late-night snack.

CAVIAR: WHAT AN ENDING
FOR 4

This little gathering is the ideal formula for winding down after an evening out on the town. Following a heavy dosage of big-city excitement, you know it's going to be difficult to get to sleep. You had a light supper hours ago, and brunch isn't until mid-morning. So why not splurge with a deluxe midnight snack featuring good-quality Russian caviar, fine French Champagne, and a few excellent cigars to top off the festivities?

Our late-night supper took place in the den of my New York City apartment just off Fifth Avenue, an enclave I call the Red Room. It is a sleek, suave, and sophisticated miniature microclimate, where four people can go to relax and insulate themselves from the commotion outside.

THE MENU: MIDNIGHT SUPPER FOR FOUR

MAIN COURSE
SMASHED POTATO WITH CAVIAR

DESSERT
CHOCOLATE MOUSSE WITH RASPBERRIES

TO DRINK
CHAMPAGNE WITH THE CAVIAR
COGNAC WITH THE DESSERT AND CIGARS

TIMING The potato takes about a half hour to boil, so you can prepare it in advance. The dessert requires refrigeration, so it, too, can be made in advance–the morning before or the afternoon of the party.

There's Nothing Like Quality: Caviar and Champagne, a Happy Marriage

Genuine caviar consists of lightly salted sturgeon eggs from the Caspian Sea. The vast majority of it is produced in Russia; a relatively small amount comes from Iran. Other types of fish eggs use the name caviar, but the term must be preceded by a qualifier —for example, "salmon caviar" or "lumpfish caviar."

There are three principal types of caviar: beluga, osetra, and sevruga. The beluga is the largest sturgeon—it can weigh up to 1,700 pounds—and produces the largest eggs (also known as "berries" or "grains" in the business) with a much-prized mild flavor. They can be as large as small peas and are gray or black in color; they are also rather fragile and can become mushy if they burst. Osetra caviar is the mid-size version; it has a stronger flavor than beluga, and its berries are yellowish gray, brownish gray, or plain old gray. The third and most common form of genuine caviar is sevruga; it has the smallest, darkest-colored, and strongest-flavored eggs. A fourth, very rare form comes from the sterlet sturgeon. It has gold-colored eggs and a mild smoky flavor, and it was traditionally reserved for the shah of Iran or the czar of Russia, depending upon which side of the Caspian it was harvested from.

Malossol is the Russian term for "a small amount of salt," which denotes high-quality caviar. The salt is added as a preservative, but caviar is still extremely perishable and must be refrigerated or vacuum-packed at all times.

When the Russian aristocracy went into exile following the revolution, many of them fled to Paris, where they introduced caviar to high society. The Petrossian brothers helped popularize it in the mid-1920s, and Monsieur Charles Ritz put it on the menu at his hotel, where it has remained ever since.

Caviar is served on bone or mother-of-pearl spoons. Why? Not just for effect. Metal-alloy utensils can ruin its taste, and silver ones can tarnish. Ice-cold vodka is one classic accompaniment for caviar; Champagne is the other. Caviar's dense richness, its distinct taste of the sea, and its saltiness are beautifully offset and balanced by the light effervescence of the bubbly. In fact, Champagne is an excellent pairing with many types of seafood.

Champagne, the other partner in this delectable marriage, comes from a designated area to the northeast of Paris, the northernmost winegrowing region of France, called (of course) Champagne. Like caviar, there are many casual usurpers of its name, but there is only one genuine article.

The millions of tiny bubbles that define Champagne's inimitable mouth-tingling texture— and make it the world's premier wine for celebrations—are the product of a second fermenta-

tion in bottle (after the primary fermentation, which is when grape sugars are converted to alcohol). Most wines give off carbon dioxide bubbles while they are aging in casks, and the gas seeps out through the porous wood. Champagne, however, is aged in bottle, so the bubbles are captured for our perpetual enjoyment.

The labor-intensive, multi-step process of blending wines for Champagne and capturing the effects of the second fermentation while minimizing the explosion of bottles was developed by a seventeenth-century Benedictine monk and master winemaker named Dom Pérignon. Champagne is one of the few wines for which the year of its production doesn't matter so much. Vintage Champagne, produced from highly selected grapes all harvested in the same year, is really superb, but it is merely the tip of the iceberg. Most Champagne is a result of careful blending of different vintages.

From the consumer's viewpoint, Champagne provides a wide range of flavors and sugar contents—from dry to sweet. It is categorized as follows: *brut* is very dry, less than 1.4 percent sugar; *extra sec* or extra dry is

up to 2 percent sugar; *sec* is 1.7 to 3.5 percent sugar; *demi-sec* is 3.3 to 5 percent sugar; and *doux* is over 5 percent.

Fine Champagne should be served at about 45°F., which is a little warmer than the temperature of your refrigerator. You can store it in the fridge and take it out a few minutes before opening the bottle, or you can chill it in a bucket with ice water, which is the quickest, most efficient method. But don't let it get too cold, as you'll miss some of its wonderful flavors.

The correct method of opening a bottle of Champagne is to hold it securely on a tabletop or counter with one hand, grip the cork with the other hand, and gently, firmly twist the bottle under the cork, applying downward pressure on the cork and easing it out of the bottle with nary a pop or fizz. Pushing or pulling the cork out suddenly to create a loud pop and fizz is unnecessary, wasteful (some precious wine can dribble out), and potentially dangerous (you could hit yourself or somebody else with the cork).

My suggestion is that you keep a bottle chilled in the fridge 24/7/365. You never know when you might have a reason to celebrate.

411: La Veuve Clicquot

Monsieur Clicquot was a successful Champagne producer in the eighteenth century. When he died prematurely, his wife took over the business and became known as "La Veuve Clicquot" (the Widow Clicquot). It was uncommon for a woman to run a business in that era, but she singlehandedly built her husband's legacy to historical proportions. In the first year, she began exporting Champagne to the czar of Russia, significantly expanding the operation. Until that time, Champagne was clouded by sediment that developed in the bottles during the fermentation process; it did not have the shimmering, clear, sparkling, golden appearance that makes it not only a treat to drink but beautiful to behold. For this reason, high-end consumers like the czars would serve it in etched or multifaceted glasses. La Veuve Clicquot developed a solution to this problem. She drilled holes in her large worktable and placed the bottles in the holes at a 45-degree angle. Then she rotated the bottles 15 degrees on their axes every day. This, she discovered, created a solid plug of sediment in the neck of each bottle, so she could later uncork her Champagne, pull out the plug of sediment, and recork it. For her achievement in perfecting the Champagne-making process, she is revered in French history, taking her place alongside Joan of Arc, Madame Curie, and just a few others.

Her bottle-rotating technique is used to this day, and very fine Champagne is still sold under her name.

OTT: A Few of the World's Finest Champagnes

Billecart-Salmon
Bollinger
Charles Heidiseck
Dom Pérignon
   (Moët & Chandon)
Krug
Laurent-Perrier
Louis Roederer (Cristal)
Mumm
Perrier-Jouët
Pol Roger
Ruinart
Taittinger
Veuve Clicquot

SMASHED POTATO WITH CAVIAR

The traditional accompaniment for caviar is a medley of toast points or melba toast, crème fraîche or sour cream, chopped egg yolks, chopped egg whites, and minced fresh white onion. Here I've created a simple variation using potato and crème fraîche, which I think really highlights the extraordinary taste and appearance of the caviar. It is an absolute must to use the highest-quality caviar possible. When you have the best-quality caviar, it is not necessary to use onions, eggs, or chives; a drop of lemon juice is sometimes the only accompaniment required.

I MEDIUM RUSSET POTATO
2 TABLESPOONS HEAVY CREAM, WARMED
I TABLESPOON UNSALTED BUTTER
FRESHLY GROUND WHITE PEPPER, TO TASTE
4 TABLESPOONS CRÈME FRAÎCHE
8 OUNCES CAVIAR (2 OUNCES PER PERSON)
CHIVES, SLICED, FOR GARNISH

1. Place the potato in a medium saucepan filled with water and bring to a boil over high heat. Reduce the heat and simmer until the potato is easily pierced with a knife, about 30 minutes. When the potato is done, drain and allow to cool. Then peel it, return it to the pot, and crush it with the tines of a large fork until it is finely textured and fluffy.
2. Warm the cream in a small saucepan over medium heat. Stir the warm cream and the butter into the potato. Season to taste with pepper.
3. Place equal amounts of the smashed potato in 4 small glass dishes and smooth the surface. Top each dish with 1 tablespoon of the crème fraîche, spreading it out to the edges of the dish to make a smooth, uniform layer. Place 2 ounces of caviar on top of each dish, garnish with chives, and serve immediately.

NOTE The caviar should be taken from the refrigerator, cold, and placed on top of the potatoes and crème fraîche immediately before serving. Caviar is fragile and perishable, and should always be refrigerated (unless, of course, it is vacuum packed).

411: Crème Fraîche

This is a traditional French dairy product that consists of mildly fermented cream. Unpasteurized cream can be fermented into crème fraîche by naturally occurring bacteria, whereas pasteurized cream requires the addition of certain lactic bacteria to be converted. Crème fraîche has a mild, tangy flavor and a consistency that ranges from that of sour cream to that of a stick of cold butter, and it can be boiled without clotting or coagulating —all properties that contribute to its usefulness and versatility. It is used extensively in French cuisine for soups, salad dressings, sauces, pastry fillings, vegetable dishes, stews, and fricasees, or as an accompaniment to fresh fruits and various other desserts. And of course it's divine with caviar!

Cigars

The occasional after-dinner cigar is truly one of life's greatest pleasures. Arguably, the world's greatest cigars come from Cuba, but unfortunately they are currently illegal for import into the United States. Alas, the great Cuban brands such as Cohiba, Partagas, Romeo y Julieta, and Montecristo are only available to us abroad. But many of the cigar-manufacturing families that were exiled during Castro's revolution have put down roots in nearby countries such as the Dominican Republic and Nicaragua—literally, because they've cultivated the Cuban tobacco seeds. They are turning out excellent cigars, and some of them are using their own brand names; so there is a Partagas brand from Cuba and another from the Dominican Republic.

Cigars sizes are designated by two numbers: the length in inches and the diameter in 64ths of an inch. In addition, each size has a nickname, the origins of which are generally obscured by the smoke and haze of Cuban history. The Corona, for example, one of the most popular sizes, is $5\frac{1}{2} \times 42$, or five and a half inches long and 42/64ths of an inch thick. The thicker a cigar, the milder and mellower it smokes. Cigar shapes are divided into two categories: parejos, which are cylindrical (with straight sides), and figurados, which have tapered sides—either at one end so they're conical (called a pyramid), or at

both ends so they're submarine-shaped (perfectos and torpedos). One of the finest cigars in the world is the genuine Cuban Montecristo No. 2, which is a conical $6\frac{1}{8} \times 52$ with a tapered smoking end. (The end that you light is called the foot; the one that you smoke is the head.) Some shapes are named after famous personages who habitually smoked them, for example the Churchill (after Sir Winston) or the Lonsdale (after the Earl). My personal favorite is the Robusto, a shortened version of the Churchill; its relative thickness gives a mild, smooth, rich smoke, and it lasts just long enough to enjoy but not too long.

Connoisseurs pride themselves on tasting their cigars as oenophiles taste wines. They can discern flavor from fruity and nutty to floral, herbal, and spicy. Cigars are rated light, medium, or heavy in terms of body; and mild, medium, and full in terms of degree of flavor. A certain cigar might be termed medium-bodied and full-flavored with notes of coffee and nutmeg. Most experts agree that the wrapper, which is the specially grown leaf in which the main body of tobacco (called the filler) is enveloped, can account for up to 60 percent of a cigar's flavors and aromas. In general, the darker the wrapper, the more full-bodied and sweeter the smoke.

Fine cigars can be kept for months—even years—if they're stored in a humidor at consistent, steady conditions of 68° to

70°F. and 70 to 72 percent humidity. Prior to lighting a cigar, you need to clip a small hole in the end you smoke. The preferred tool for this is a small guillotine (cigar cutter); in a pinch, you could use a small, sharp pair of scissors or a very sharp paring knife. Some connoisseurs will tell you never to touch the end of the cigar to the flame when lighting; the keys are to light it with a strong, steady, neutral (gas-free) flame and to rotate the cigar so the entire end is lit evenly. A superior, hand-rolled cigar can last up to 45 minutes. Most connoisseurs will only smoke about the first half, as it begins to turn harsher when it burns down.

411: Classic Cigar Sizes and Shapes

Churchill: 7×48 or 49
Corona: $5\frac{1}{2} \times 42$
Double Corona:
$\quad 7\frac{1}{2}$ to 8×49 to 52
Lonsdale: $6\frac{1}{4}$ to $6\frac{1}{2} \times$
$\quad 42$ to 44
Panatela: 5 to $7\frac{1}{2} \times 33$ to 38
Petit Corona: $4\frac{1}{2} \times 40$ to 42
Robusto: 5 to $5\frac{1}{2} \times 50$

411: Recommended Cigar Brands

Arturo Fuente, Davidoff,
El Rey del Mundo,
H. Upmann, Hoyo de
Monterrey, Licenciados
Macanudo, Montecristo,
Partagas, Punch, Ramon
Allones, Romeo y Julieta

Chocolate Mousse with Raspberries

Here is an elegant dessert that I always think of as originating in the 1950s. I've heightened and lightened it, respectively, by serving it in elegant martini glasses and garnishing it with fresh raspberries.

4 1/2 ounces good-quality bittersweet chocolate

1 stick (1/2 cup) unsalted butter

4 large eggs, separated

1/4 cup sugar

1 6-ounce container of fresh raspberries, for garnish

1 bunch of fresh mint, for garnish

1. Place the chocolate and butter in a bain-marie or double boiler over medium heat and, stirring occasionally, melt until smooth. Remove from the heat, allow to cool, and transfer to a large mixing bowl.
2. Place the egg yolks and half of the sugar in a separate mixing bowl, and whisk together until creamy. Set aside.
3. Place the egg whites in the bowl of an electric mixer and mix until they form soft peaks, gradually adding the remaining sugar while mixing.
4. Fold the egg-yolk mixture into the chocolate and blend well. Using a spatula, gently fold in the egg-white mixture until well incorporated. Refrigerate for 2 to 3 hours, until ready to serve.
5. To serve, place the mousses in individual martini glasses, then top with raspberries and a fresh mint leaf.

Resources

A lot of readers might be puzzled or stumped as to where I get some of the more interesting and at times uncommon items— objets d'art, if you will—for my table arrangements. Well, these days it's becoming easier and easier to find an incredible global range of items at the large houseware stores and through their catalogs. Try Bed, Bath & Beyond; Pier 1 Imports; Global Table in Manhattan's SoHo district; Pottery Barn; Crate & Barrel; Williams-Sonoma, and others like them. You'd be surprised how many fun, serendipitous items you'll come across once you start looking. Collect all kinds of mail-order catalogs, go to flea markets, visit the African street vendors you find in just about any city in the world now. For companies with multiple locations, call on the phone or visit their websites to determine the location nearest you.

Food & Wine Purveyors

Bel Air Caviar Merchant *(for the best caviar)*
10423 Santa Monica Boulevard, Los Angeles, CA 90025-5604
Phone: 310-474-9518

Dean & Deluca
Phone: 877-826-9246
Website: www.deandeluca.com
E-mail: atyourservice@deandeluca.com

Eli's Vinegar Factory
431 East 91st Street, New York, NY 10129
Phone: 212-987-0885

Joe's Stone Crab
11 Washington Avenue, Miami, FL 33139
Phone: 800-260-CRAB
Website: www.joestonecrab.com
E-mail: QandA@joestonecrab.com

Kalustyan's Orient Expert Trading Comany
(for Indian spices, pappadums, etc.)
123 Lexington Avenue, New York, NY 10016
Phone: 212-685-3451
Website: www.kalystayans.com

Sherry Lehmann Fine Wines & Spirits
679 Madison Avenue, New York, NY 10021
Phone: 212-838-7500
Website: www.sherry-lehmann.com

Urbani *(for truffles, caviar, and fine foods)*
29-24 40th Avenue, Long Island City, NY 11101
Phone: 800-281-2300
Website: www.urbani.com

Fine China & Glassware

A La Maison
1078 Madison Avenue, New York, NY 10028
Phone: 212-396-1020

Baccarat
Phone: 866-886-8003
Website: www.baccarat.fr/

Michael C. Fina
545 Fifth Avenue, New York, NY 10017
Phone: 800-289-3462
Website: www.michaelcfina.com
E-mail: infor@michaelcfina.com

Wedgwood
Phone: 800-955-1550
Website: www.wedgwood.com
E-mail: feedback@wedgwood.com

Home Furnishings and Accessories

ABC Carpet & Home (Flagship Store)
881 and 888 Broadway (at 19th Street), New York, NY 10003
Phone: 212-473-3000
Website: www.abchome.com

Barney's New York
Phone: 888-222-7639
Website: www.barneys.com

Bed, Bath & Beyond
Phone: 800-462-3966
Website: www.bedbathandbeyond.com

Bergdorf Goodman
754 Fifth Avenue, New York, NY 10019
Phone: 800-964-8619

Crate & Barrel
Phone: 800-967-6696
Website: www.crateandbarrel.com

Global Table
107-109 Sullivan Street, New York, NY 10012
Phone: 212-431-5839

Pier 1 Imports
Phone: 800-245-4595
Website: www.pier1.com

Pottery Barn
Phone: 888-779-5176
Website: www.potterybarn.com

Takashimaya
Phone: 888-753-2038
Website: www.takashimaya.com

The Terrance Conran Shop
Phone: 212-755-9079
Website: www.conran.com

Williams-Sonoma
Phone: 877-812-6235
Website: www.williams-sonoma.com

Linens

Lulu DK
Phone: 212-223-4234
Website: www.luludk.com

Pratesi
Phone: 212-288-2315
Website: www.pratesi.com
E-mail: pratesiusa@pratesi.com

Miscellaneous

Claws on Wheels, Seafood Catering (for clambakes)
Based in East Hampton, N.Y.; ranging all over Long Island
Phone: 631-329-3622

Oriental Trading Company
Phone: 800-228-2269
Website: www.orientaltrading.com
If you're looking for hula skirts, miniature umbrellas for your tropical drinks, or hundreds of other fun party favors for every season and holiday, this is the catalog to check out.

Perks Peri-Peri Sauce (African Heat)
Phone: 888-737-5773
Website: www.perskperi-peri.com

Bella Cucina Artful Food (Preserved Lemons)
Phone: 800-580-5674

ACKNOWLEDGMENTS

One of my last and most pleasurable tasks in completing this book is acknowledging everyone involved and saying thank you. It's been a happy experience that brings to mind lots of spontaneous laughter and wonderful memories. A project like this takes a gazillion phone calls and many favors. A large amount of work was concentrated in a short period of time, and I couldn't be happier with the results. To work and collaborate with such gifted people is both a treat and a blessing.

I have thoroughly enjoyed working with my editor, a true professional who passionately believed in this project, Chris Pavone at Clarkson Potter. I thank Quentin Bacon for capturing my work on film; his photography is sexy and playful. Thank you to Julie Skarratt for the pictures of Carayes in the "A Taste of Mexico" chapter and to Alec Hemer for the pictures in the "Sex on the Beach" chapter. And thanks to my agent, Margret McBride.

Writing with David Gibbons has been a true delight. His knowledge and ability to capture my voice are evident and appreciated. Cooking with Martin Herold is always an adventure; he is an extraordinarily gifted chef. To my business partner, David Berke, and to my associates in the New York and Los Angeles offices who all worked on this project, thank you: Sarah Zamor, Alicia Graham, Laine Sutton, Nicole Paige, Gertrude Kleszczewski, and Eva Klewszczewski. I am also thankful for my lifelong friend, the gifted designer Charles Allem, for his great eye, brutal honesty, and constant inspiration. And thanks to my partner in life and in business, Stuart Brownstein, for his help in making this project come together and his never-ending support.

For the phenomenal homes and locations, I am most grateful to: Kalliope Karella and Michael Rena, John Barman and Kelly Graham, Lulu De Kwiatkowski, Jim Block, Sloan and Roger Barnett, Kai and Doron Linz, Regan Silber, Michael Dubelko and Dagny Hultgreen, Kevin Wendle, Geoffrey Bradfield, and Elizabeth and Lars Enochson. Thanks for making us so welcome and giving us such beautiful canvases to bring alive and capture our work. Thank you to a few great stores that were very generous: Tesoro in Beverly Hills, Michael C. Fina in New York City, Baccarat in New York City, Lenox Brands in Lawrenceville, A La Maison in New York City, Crate & Barrel in New York City, Van Cleef & Arpels in New York City, and Wedgwood U.S.A.

And finally, to my mother, Gloria Cowie, for always being an extraordinary force and influence in my life. I've never met anyone filled with more love and kindness.

Index

CONVERSION CHART
Equivalent Imperial and Metric Measurements

American cooks use standard containers, the 8-ounce cup and a tablespoon that takes exactly 16 level fillings to fill that cup level. Measuring by cup makes it very difficult to give weight equivalents, as a cup of densely packed butter will weigh considerably more than a cup of flour. The easiest way therefore to deal with cup measurements in recipes is to take the amount by volume rather than by weight. Thus the equation reads:

1 cup = 240 ml = 8 fl. oz.   ½ cup = 120 ml = 4 fl. oz.

It is possible to buy a set of American cup measures in major stores around the world.

In the States, butter is often measured in sticks. One stick is the equivalent of 8 tablespoons. One tablespoon of butter is therefore the equivalent to ½ ounce/15 grams.

LIQUID MEASURES

Fluid Ounces	U.S.	Imperial	Milliliters
	1 teaspoon	1 teaspoon	5
¼	2 teaspoons	1 dessertspoon	10
½	1 tablespoon	1 tablespoon	14
1	2 tablespoons	2 tablespoons	28
2	¼ cup	4 tablespoons	56
4	½ cup		110
5		¼ pint or 1 gill	140
6	¾ cup		170
8	1 cup		225
9			250, ¼ liter
10	1¼ cups	½ pint	280
12	1½ cups		340
15		¾ pint	420
16	2 cups		450
18	2¼ cups		500, ½ liter
20	2½ cups	1 pint	560
24	3 cups		675
25		1¼ pints	700
27	3½ cups		750
30	3¾ cups	1½ pints	840
32	4 cups or 1 quart		900
35		1¾ pints	980
36	4½ cups		1000, 1 liter
40	5 cups	2 pints or 1 quart	1120

SOLID MEASURES

U.S. and Imperial Measures		Metric Measures	
Ounces	Pounds	Grams	Kilos
1		28	
2		56	
3½		100	
4	¼	112	
5		140	
6		168	
8	½	225	
9		250	¼
12	¾	340	
16	1	450	
18		500	½
20	1¼	560	
24	1½	675	
27		750	¾
28	1¾	780	
32	2	900	
36	2¼	1000	1
40	2½	1100	
48	3	1350	
54		1500	1½

OVEN TEMPERATURE EQUIVALENTS

Fahrenheit	Celsius	Gas Mark	Description
225	110	¼	Cool
250	130	½	
275	140	1	Very Slow
300	150	2	
325	170	3	Slow
350	180	4	Moderate
375	190	5	
400	200	6	Moderately Hot
425	220	7	Fairly Hot
450	230	8	Hot
475	240	9	Very Hot
500	250	10	Extremely Hot

Any broiling recipes can be used with the grill of the oven, but beware of high-temperature grills.

EQUIVALENTS FOR INGREDIENTS

all-purpose flour—plain flour	half and half—12% fat milk	scallion—spring onion
coarse salt—kitchen salt	heavy cream—double cream	unbleached flour—strong, white flour
cornstarch—cornflour	light cream—single cream	zest—rind
eggplant—aubergine	lima beans—broad beans	zucchini—courgettes or marrow